The Problem of the Lord's Supper

The Problem of the Lord's Supper
according to the Scholarly Research
of the Nineteenth Century
and the Historical Accounts

Volume 1

The Lord's Supper in Relationship to the Life of Jesus and the History of the Early Church

by Albert Schweitzer

translated by A. J. Mattill, Jr.

edited with an introduction by John Reumann

Mercer University
Press
Macon, Ga. 31207

Originally published as
*Das Abendmahlsproblem auf Grund der wissenschaftlichen Forschung
des 19. Jahrhunderts und der historischen Berichte*
Heft 1: *Das Abendmahl im Zusammenhang mit dem Leben Jesu
und der Geschichte des Urchristentums*
by J. C. B. Mohr (Paul Siebeck), Tübingen, in 1901,
the present English translation is from the
Zweite, photomechanisch gedruckte Auflage (1929),
by arrangement with J. C. B. Mohr (Paul Siebeck).

All books published by Mercer University Press are produced
on acid-free paper which exceeds the minimum standards set by the
National Historical Publications and Records Commission.

Library of Congress Cataloging in Publication Data

Schweitzer, Albert, 1875-1965.
   The problem of the Lord's Supper according to the scholarly research of the nineteenth century and the historical accounts.

   Translation of: Das Abendmahlsproblem auf Grund der wissenschaftlichen Forschung des 19. Jahrhunderts und der historischen Berichte. 2. Aufl. 1929. (Das Abendmahl im Zusammenhang mit dem Leben Jesu und der Geschichte des Urchristentums; heft 1)
   Bibliography: p. 39.
   Includes indexes.
   1. Lord's Supper—History—19th century.

I. Reumann, John Henry Paul.   II. Title.
BV823.S2913   232.9′57   81-22590
ISBN 0-86554-025-X   AACR2

Table of Contents

Editor's Preface

The importance of this basic work on the Lord's Supper by Albert Schweitzer (1875-1965), produced in 1900 as his doctoral dissertation in New Testament studies, is set forth in the Introduction below. There is also provided there an account of its place in Schweitzer's career overall, an analysis of the contents, and some assessment of what the twenty-five-year-old theologian achieved in this initial venture into biblical scholarship.

A recently published international bibliography on Schweitzer by Nancy Snell Griffith and Laura Person (see below, p. 40, for this title, and for others mentioned subsequently) confirms what is claimed in the Introduction—that Schweitzer's 1901 publication (on the Lord's Supper in relationship to the life of Jesus and the history of the early church) is herewith being translated from the original German for the first time into any language. The Griffith-Person listing also indicates that virtually no attention (compared with his other writings) has been given, even in German scholarship, to this book of Schweitzer except for references noted on pages 2, 28, and 29 below, and in the thesis (not available to me) by Bruno Ognibeni at the University of Freiburg in 1971, "Das Abendmahlsproblem in exegetischem Werk von Albert Schweitzer. Eine methodologische Forschung."

The contention of the Introduction is that this early volume by Schweitzer was pivotal for his own development, a kind of blueprint for future work. It was also to prove in its own way, at least indirectly, strangely—and, indeed, ecumenically—influential for current thought and praxis involving the Lord's Supper even if it must be admitted that Schweitzer's attempt here to link Jesus' last supper with the Lord's Supper of the early church did not carry the day in New Testament studies. But it may be added that his bold attempt to find verisimilitude for eucharistic origins in the words and actions of Jesus in the upper room as reported by Mark, even though by and large rejected in much subsequent scholarship, still flourishes in views found in some quite recent treatments like that of the German Catholic exegete Rudolf Pesch (see below, p. 41). Schweitzer's answer, that Mark's account must be regarded as *the* authentic one, thus still has its followers. Indeed, eighty years later, the case for Mark to be representing Jesus' own intentions is being argued as vigorously now as by Schweitzer then, though with some different nuances.

The Introduction describes (p. 3) how the present translation has belatedly—as with so much scholarly landmark literature in German on the New Testament—come into English at this time. It is a pleasure to pay tribute to the initiative that Dr. Watson Mills and Mr. Edd Rowell, of Mercer University Press, took in seeking out the rights to the Schweitzer volume for translation, and in securing the services of Dr. A. J. Mattill, Jr. as translator. The latter's prompt rendering has been, in consultation with the translator, revised and edited by Mr. Edd Rowell, Editor-in-Chief of the Press. Dr. Mills and Mr. Rowell also have been responsible for the Indexes, a welcome addition to the German original.

As author of the interpretative essay which appears as the Introduction (pp. 1-37), I have also been responsible for preparing this Preface and for certain notes added to the translation of Schweitzer's work.

So that the mechanics are clear, let it be noted that all *numbered* footnotes in the thirteen chapters of Schweitzer's volume (pp. 43-137 below) are the work of Albert Schweitzer himself, and have been reproduced in translation exactly as he himself had them originally, abbreviations and all. Schweitzer's dissertation included only eighteen such notes (e.g., especially on pp. 65-66 and, regarding textual matters, pp. 116-18); elsewhere he made precise the location of materials being discussed by citing title, date, and pages in the body of the dissertation itself (e.g., pp. 66-68). As there was no bibliography, these two methods constituted Schweitzer's reference system for the technical literature which he took up.

For the convenience of readers I have added additional information, chiefly about scholars cited and more precise reference to their works, especially (where such exists) in English translations, including what Schweitzer may have said on them elsewhere. These additions are always indicated with the initials "J. R." In the Preface and Part One, Chapter I, these additions from the editor are indicated by the use of one or more *asterisks* at the pertinent phrase or name and are printed at the bottom of the page. Beginning with Chapter III these editor's additions are inserted *within brackets* at the start of the section where a given author is discussed (e.g., pp. 65, 66, 67, 68), and once again initialed "J. R." This style reflects the method used by Schweitzer himself in the 1906 book on the quest and in his history of Pauline scholarship (1911). In rare cases (e.g., p. 66, fn. 4) he tells us a bit about a writer himself, thus foreshadowing his own later technique. In such instances I have not added any more details in an editor's note.

Though in his later years Schweitzer moved into more philosophical matters and gave himself to concerns such as, for example, the use of atomic weaponry, the facts that Schweitzer wrote on the Lord's Supper as he did in this book and, as a theologian and a modern saint, has been etched in stained glass in some churches (such as the Chapel of Mansfield College, Oxford), and as a missionary and thinker, has been given a place in some ecclesiastical calendars as a "renewer of the church," makes it proper, I believe, to raise some practical and ecumenical questions to which this youthful dissertation of his points. This I sought to do briefly below (pp. 34-37) and more fully elsewhere (cf. the lecture alluded to on p. 41, *s.v.* 'Pesch").

J. R.

Introduction

by John Reumann

Introduction

by
John Reumann
Lutheran Theological Seminary, Philadelphia, Pa.

The translation which follows, for the first time in English, is of Albert Schweitzer's 1900 dissertation for the licentiate degree in theology, including his exegesis on the Lord's Supper texts in the New Testament and in Justin Martyr, as published in 1901. This appearance in translation is no belated commemoration of the hundredth anniversary of Schweitzer's birth, celebrated in 1975 (he died in 1965), nor a salute to the seventy-fifth anniversary of his famed book on the quest of the historical Jesus, the first edition of which came out in German in 1906 (although it is appropriate to mark that milestone by publication in translation—at last—of the book which generated Schweitzer's work on Jesus).

This appearance in English garb of Schweitzer's often terse German volume could be justified as delayed attention to one of the few remaining major bits of Schweitzeriana not yet available in translation. But in actuality a case can be made for calling new attention to it afresh in any language, German included, because of the comparative neglect of this initial treatise by Schweitzer on the New Testament. The massive treatment of Schweitzer as scholar and thinker by Helmut Groos in 1974[1], in its more than 230 pages on Schweitzer's *Leben-Jesu-Forschung*, does not deal with this seminal essay. Erich Grässer's definitive treatment on Schweitzer as theologian (1979) provides 25 pages (out of 267 in his text) on Schweitzer and the "problem of the Lord's Supper," and any subsequent discussion of the matter is in Professor Grässer's debt. Yet even Grässer is unable to report much attention to Schweitzer's first 1901 publication by subsequent writers on either the New Testament or the history of the development of the Christian "sacrament of the altar."

More specifically, Schweitzer's 1901 book on *Das Abendmahls-problem* (even the title is something of a challenge, for, since it means literally "evening meal," it can refer both to what we call "the last supper" of Jesus with the twelve and to the holy communion or Eucharist or church sacrament which developed in early Christianity) has value for the insights it gives into his early development as a graduate student and his approach to scholarly problems. It provides an interesting analysis of understandings of the Lord's Supper from the time of Zwingli to about 1900, when Schweitzer wrote his treatise. Indeed his "typology" of the sacrament offers an analysis unutilized by most sacramentalogists and worth testing by church historians and students of dogma. The book also offers, we shall suggest, the most detailed exegesis of any New Testament passages ever published by Schweitzer. Above all, the book shows us the road through which Schweitzer came to his reconstruction of an eschatological, dogmatic Jesus, presented in Mark's gospel. The road to this Jesus led for Schweitzer through the upper room.

Along with all these reasons for making Schweitzer's pages available to a wider audience in English, there must be noted also a further effect: *Das Abendmahlsproblem* raises questions, about Schweitzer, about his research and attitudes and about our understandings of the last/Lord's Supper. Some of these questions we shall note in the

---

[1]Bibliographical items will be identified in this introduction in a short form by the author's name and/or a short title, and where necessary the year and place of publication. Full bibliographical information appears below, on pages 39-42.

Introduction, and in some cases give suggestions toward answers. Ultimately we shall be faced by the question with which Schweitzer wrestled: how does what Jesus said and did in the upper room relate to what Christians after Easter came to understand about bread and wine, as they received each in the Lord's Supper? To be concerned with such matters brings us beyond historical questions to questions of practical and even ecumenical concern in Christendom.

In seeking to set all these matters in perspective and thus aid appreciation and even comprehension of Schweitzer's own words, we shall in this Introduction deal first with Schweitzer's career generally and his work as a New Testament scholar, including the place of the *Abendmahlsproblem* essay. Then we shall look more closely at Schweitzer's essay itself. (If that seems unnecessary duplication when one can read for oneself below what Schweitzer said, our defense is that Schweitzer's words in German are close-packed words, not easy to put into smooth-flowing English. It has been said that the roughness of his German in its Alsatian patois form became smoother later on after his association with Hélène Bresslau, a professor's daughter whom he later married, and with other friends.) Then we shall indicate how the 1901 essay served as impetus for Schweitzer's later work on the quest and on Paul, within the framework of what he laid out in 1900 in the pages of the book before us. Finally we shall try to assess Schweitzer's achievements on the problem of the Lord's Supper in terms of his avowed aims and, at least to some degree, of later scholarship, and we shall note the questions that loom partially unanswered for further thought.

Impetus for this translation arose especially out of a paper of my own on the topic presented to the Studiorum Novi Testamenti Societas, meeting in Toronto, Canada, in 1980, and subsequently published in its journal. (That paper grew in turn out of my own long-term study of Schweitzer and the quest for the historical Jesus.) The difficult task of trying to make Schweitzer speak English has been the lot of Dr. A. J. Mattill, Jr., of Gordo, Alabama, known for his rendering of the 1966 edition in English of Feine-Behm-Kümmel's *Introduction to the New Testament* and his work on Luke-Acts. Notes that I have supplied to the translation are signed "J. R."

The text translated below is that of the second edition, photomechanically reproduced in 1929 from the original 1901 printing by the same publisher, J. C. B. Mohr (Paul Siebeck), Tübingen, with the permission of Herr Siebeck.

I. The Context in Schweitzer's Career

Given the many interests, talents, and indeed careers of Albert Schweitzer, it probably is not surprising that he wrote a book on the Lord's Supper. After all, his very first publication in 1898 had been on music, in honor of one of his teachers, Eugène Muench (uncle of the later conductor in Boston, Charles Muench), and his doctor's dissertation in 1899 had been on the philosophy of Immanuel Kant. Why not a book on the last supper and holy communion? But that is to get ahead of the story. Some reminders of Schweitzer's amazing and versatile life are needed as context for his career in biblical studies. We concentrate here on aspects pertinent to the volume on *Das Abendmahlsproblem.*

Schweitzer's Life

Born at Kaysersburg, Albert Schweitzer was the son of one Lutheran clergyman and the grandson on his mother's side of another. Young Albert was named for a third minister, Albert Schillinger (half brother of his mother), who had been pastor of the St. Nicholas Church in Strassburg—where, as the Rev. Albert Schweitzer, he too was later to serve several times. Thus the study of theology was almost inevitable. The theological environment of his family and the times was that of rural Evangelical piety and Protestant liberalism.

He grew up at Günsbach, another town south of Strassburg, where his father was then pastor. Gymnasium studies were at Mulhouse, not far away. Cultural horizons were in part set by Colmar, with its museum housing the famous Grünewald altar. When time came for university studies, these were available in the spanking new buildings and faculties at Strassburg, again not far away. Even if we include travels to study music in France and trips to Oberammergau for the Passion Play and to Bayreuth to hear his beloved Wagner's *Ring Cycle*, Schweitzer's life, until he went to Africa as a missionary, was almost entirely limited to the area between Paris and Berlin, concentrated around Strassburg. Even his army duty in 1894-1895 was done nearby.

To family faith and Alsatian environment we must add German culture and *Wissenschaft* and pride in such things German as part of Schweitzer's background. True, Alsace had become German (again) only after the Franco-Prussian War in 1870-1871. But young Schweitzer, while maintaining something of his dual heritage, enthused to the achievements of German scholarship at the university, as his autobiography and writings show. His way of posing problems theological and philosophical will root in German Reformation and subsequent Protestant thought.

Aptitude for music led to mastering the organ under one good teacher after another until, beginning in 1893, even before he entered the university, Schweitzer was studying under the great Charles Marie Widor in Paris. Widor encouraged him to write a pamphlet on Bach which, at Schweitzer's hand, turned into a French biography in 1905, an even bigger German edition in 1908, and five volumes on Bach's organ works. As is well known, Schweitzer performed at the organ all over Europe during his long career. As is less well known, he also published in 1906 a standard booklet on organ building.

His academic career at Strassburg (summer semester, 1899, in Berlin) began in 1893. By 1899 he had earned the doctor in philosophy degree, with a dissertation on Kant's *Critique of Pure Reason.* As we shall detail below, he secured his licentiate in theology the next year, and by 1901 had published the required further dissertation (on Jesus, in light of his last supper research which is translated below) that opened the door to a teaching career. Schweitzer lectured in the Protestant theology faculty at Strassburg from 1902 until early 1912.

One could also detail for this period a career as administrator (as principal of the Theological College, 1903-1906) and pastor (at the Nikolaikirche), as well as his resolve, made known to friends in 1905, to study medicine and go to Africa as a mission doctor. Suffice to say he did give a lifetime of service at Lambaréné in what was then French Equatorial Africa, 1913-1917, 1924-1927, 1929-1932, 1933, and on until his death. Somehow Schweitzer found time to seek a wife and marry, in 1912. After one sojourn in Africa Frau Schweitzer lived mostly in Germany, at Königsfeld, Schwarzwald. One daughter, Rhena, was born to them in 1919.

To these careers in music, theology, medicine, and missions, we could add, among his other pursuits, books on the philosophy of civilization and world religions; books of sermons; essays on Goethe and ethics; urgent appeals about the dangers from the atom bomb for world peace; not to mention autobiographical and even devotional writings. But all these aspects of his life already enumerated are probably enough to recall the many-sidedness of Schweitzer, of which his biblical research was but a part.

The Work of Schweitzer as New Testament Scholar

The versatile and able boy from Günsbach entered the university at age 18. The year from April 1894 until April 1895 was taken up with service as an army conscript. But even that time was productive, for, as Schweitzer tells us in *Out of My Life and Thought* (pp. 17-20)—in what are no doubt selectively recorded anecdotes written up some thirty-five years later—it was on army maneuvers that Schweitzer stumbled onto "eschatology" as a neglected clue in Jesus' life. This clue arose for him from the statement in Matthew 10:23, where we are told that Jesus sent the twelve disciples out to preach and warned them of persecution: "Truly, I say to you, you will not have gone through all the towns of Israel before the Son of man comes." The fact was, as Schweitzer read in Mark 6:30, the apocalyptic Son of man did *not* come then, for the twelve returned safely to Jesus. But Schweitzer was alerted to look at other references to "the Son of man," at apocalyptic imagery ("revealings" of the "last times," for that is what "eschatology" denotes) embedded in Mark, Matthew, and Luke. Schweitzer reasoned that no one would have invented *un*fulfilled predictions and put them on Jesus' lips; therefore such statements as Matthew 10:23 must be authentic. They were therefore genuine aspects of Jesus' outlook which the liberal portraits of the day did not assimilate into their summary of him as "teacher."

A second fateful step in Schweitzer's evolution as a New Testament scholar came during his student days in 1897. While he begins his preface to the work translated below with reference to it, a fuller narrative account is provided in *Out of My Life and Thought* (pp. 24-26). For the first theological examination (which he completed 6 May 1898), Schweitzer at the close of the summer semester in 1897 found the assigned topic to be on *das Abendmahl*. The teaching of the early nineteenth-century theologian, Friedrich Ernst Daniel Schleiermacher, was to be presented and compared with concepts of the Lord's Supper laid down in the New Testament and in the Reformation confessional writings. One had eight weeks to prepare a thesis on this, which determined whether or not permission would be given to stand for the examination.

In both accounts of the incident, in our 1901 volume and autobiographically years later, Schweitzer emphasizes how he had to dig into the texts of the New Testament and the Lutheran Book of Concord, and so forth, but above all into the pertinent section of Schleiermacher's dogmatics, *The Christian Faith (Abendmahlsproblem*, p. v; below, p. 45-46).[2] The observation by Schleiermacher which particularly caught his eye was the statement that in Matthew and Mark, Jesus gives no command to repeat the rite. That is, while 1 Corinthians 11:24 and 25 have the command "Do this in remembrance of me" after the words about the bread and the words about the cup, and while Luke 22:19 (in most manuscripts but not all) has "Do this in remembrance of me" after the saying about the bread (but not in v. 20 in connection with the cup; RSV puts 22:19*b* and 20 in small type as a footnote), neither Mark (cf. 14:22-24) nor Matthew (cf. 26:26-28) has any command to "do this" hereafter with bread and with wine. Schleiermacher had not really made anything much of this observation, but it set Schweitzer thinking, as he worked through the *Abendmahl* materials for his examination.

Schweitzer's 1901 preface (pp. vi-vii; below, pp. 46-47) cited Schleiermacher's paragraph in *Der christliche Glaube* at length, including the key phrases indicated by that Germanic device of spaced letters (italicized here):

> This consideration [that thc Lord's Supper can no more be what Christ instituted and may well not have been ordained by him as a permanent institution for the church]. . . *can now readily make itself better known in the Evangelical Church than previously has been the case* . . . . It can hardly be maintained *that this intention* [to institute a permanent rite] *emanates distinctly from the words of Christ* . . . . [Given] *no such command* (Mark and Matthew) . . . , the apostles . . . *would have no more had the right to make a[n]* . . . *institution out of the Abendmahl* . . . than they did out of the foot-washing.

Schweitzer added, therefore, more boldly, "Our celebration of the Lord's Supper does not rest, in the final analysis, on an explicit command of Jesus." The next six pages show how he reflected upon that observation. His later account is even more direct: no current explanation of the Lord's Supper makes clear why the early Christian community had adopted the practice of the last supper, even though there had been no command from Jesus to "do this." Therefore, he will

---

[2]Hereafter references to Schweitzer's *Abendmahlsproblem* will be cited first by the page(s) of the German edition and then by the page(s) in the translation below.

conclude, all these current explanations must be wrong. Yet there must have been "something in the essence" of that last supper, "apart from the words and actions of Jesus" to have made the apostles "do this" (*Out of My Life and Thought*, pp. 25-26).

These ideas simmered as Schweitzer turned to philosophy to do a quick doctorate on Kant. The summer of 1898, after passing the First Theological Examination and earning a scholarship good for six years of further study, was spent at work in Strassburg. In October he went to Paris, partly to study organ with Widor. (After reading Kant all night, he sometimes went to a session at the console with his teacher without ever having been to bed!) In March he read a satisfactory thesis draft to his professor, Theobald Ziegler. Schweitzer enjoyed the summer semester (April-June) of 1899 in Berlin (lectures, organs, reading). The D.Phil. degree was granted in July 1899, and his analysis of how part of Kant's *Critique of Pure Reason* incorporated part of an earlier essay by Kant was published that same year.

But Schweitzer decided that teaching philosophy, even though the post of *Privat-dozent* (authorized lecturer) beckoned, was not for him. This was in part because Professor Ziegler had hinted that for a career in philosophy he ought not to be active as a preacher too. But Schweitzer dearly loved his parish work in the staff ministry at St. Nicholas, where he was appointed as *Vikar* in December 1899, and eventually was ordained as a *Pfarrer* in September 1900. Ordination came only after the Second Theological Examination which he passed on 15 July 1900—but barely, because in his work on his thesis which we are considering, he had failed to bone up on practical theology— "only just passed," as he puts it. Reminiscences of work with his fellow pastors, the orthodox but pietistic Knittel and the liberal Gerold, are recounted in *Out of My Life and Thought* (pp. 36-41), as is the most embarrassing part of the final theological examination for ordination. Pressed on the authorship of a particular hymn—it was by Karl Johann Philipp Spitta—Schweitzer replied the hymn was too insignificant to know the author! To the horror of all, the hymnwriter's son, Professor Friedrich Spitta, co-founder of the *Monatsschrift für Gottesdienst und kirchliche Kunst* (whom we shall meet later for his work on the Lord's Supper), was sitting there as one of the examiners!

Beginning on the Lord's Supper

As indicated, Schweitzer, in the latter half of 1899, had decided for theology, not philosophy (though he was to come back to the field in later books). That meant completing work for the licentiate degree in theology by 1904, in order to meet the terms of his fellowship. Schweitzer, typically, rushed ahead so as to obtain the degree as quickly as possible, in a spirit of "misplaced consideration for others," as he calls it; for he wanted to pass the scholarship on to another student, Jäger—who, however, made no use of it! The twenty-five-year-old Schweitzer obtained the degree, *magna cum laude*, on 21 July 1900. The subject of his thesis, published in 1901, was "A Critical Presentation of Diverse, New, Historical Concepts of the Lord's Supper," in essence Part I of the volume translated below. The subject, including the word "concepts" *(Auffassungen)* was an outgrowth of his work in 1897 on Schleiermacher and the *Abendmahl*.

Schweitzer thus wrote this survey of recent concepts of the meal in 1899-1900 while serving in a parish church, preaching short (less than twenty-minute) Sunday afternoon sermons and teaching confirmation classes; preparing (not as thoroughly) for his Second Exam for ordination; playing the organ; and, one suspects, doing lectures and numerous other things (cf. *Out of My Life and Thought*, pp. 38-44). He lived at the Theological College near St. Thomas' Church, the Collegium Wilhelmitanum, where he had resided as a student earlier.

But Schweitzer's research activity did not end with the licentiate thesis or even its publication, for, obedient to a grand scholarly vision, he worked on, treating also the Lord's Supper texts in the New Testament (Mark 14:22-26; Matthew 26:26-29; Luke 22:14-20; 1 Cor. 11:23-26) and in the writings of apologist Justin Martyr (mid-second century, but significant). This material was published as Part II of the volume translated below.

The study on diverse concepts of the *Abendmahl* and on the early Christian texts themselves gave birth, as we shall see, to a new view of Jesus for Schweitzer, indeed demanded "a new life of Jesus," as he concluded in his study of the Lord's Supper problem. This he tackled in a further volume, a bit longer than the two-part treatise we are presenting here, "a sketch of the life of Jesus," as he subtitled it, dealing with "the messianic- and passion-secret (or mystery)." He published this further volume along with the one before us in 1901. The second volume of 1901 served for Schweitzer as *Habilitationsschrift*, that is, a second doctoral thesis (on top of his licentiate dissertation), earning the right to appointment as *Privatdozent* in the German university system. Schweitzer received this habilitation from Strassburg in 1902, and he began, on 1 March 1902, with an inaugural lecture concerning the Logos doctrine in the Fourth Gospel. His first course of lectures, in the winter semester of 1902-1903, dealt, oddly enough, with none of his previous concerns but with the Catholic Epistles, and the next term with the Apocalypse of John.

We have mentioned Schweitzer's comprehensive scholarly vision. We shall summarize this next and then show in outline form what got written and what never did, and how the series of titles above fit in, and how his later writings build on this grand scheme.

In the 1897 encounter with Schleiermacher and his study of the early Christian and Reformation texts about the Lord's Supper, not only did Schweitzer find his appetite whetted on a topic with which he had not busied himself previously and to research on which he was in no wise oriented; but also, as he worked through the materials with his lead from Schleiermacher, the broad strokes for a new interpretation, he tells us, were outlined in his mind (1901 preface, pp. v and vii; below, pp. 45 and 48). For the next four years, he says, he studied the problem of the Lord's Supper in all epochs (ibid., p. viii; below, p. 48). That would have been from 1897 until 1901. But the solution, he insists, he had arrived at already in the fall of 1897, independent of his later examination of modern research (ibid.). Happily, this work fitted well with his discovery in 1894 of the "eschatological clue." The two questions (p. x; below, p. 50)—Why did the first Christian community observe a celebration like that associated with Jesus' last meal? and Are its reasons still valid for us?—moved Schweitzer into a broad historical, theological program.

Put briefly, Schweitzer will argue that there was no command by Jesus to repeat a meal. But the Marcan account is historically correct, with its eschatological emphasis. The focus was on Jesus' impending passion *and* his expectation to drink the fruit of the vine "new in the kingdom of God" (14:25), *not* on the "words of institution" (14:22, 24, "This is my body," "This is my blood . . ."), over which there has been so much dispute in the history of theology.

Looking backwards from the upper room, this analysis of Mark maintains that Jesus that night acted as "suffering messiah." He had a secret not shared even with many of his disciples, namely the secret of his messiahship and the secret of his passion, that only his death could serve as the necessary condition for the future reunion he expected

(14:25). That also meant a whole new way of looking at the historical Jesus: "A new life of Jesus: that is the only way to the solution to the problem of the Lord's Supper," as Schweitzer concludes Part II (p. 62; below, p. 137). In obedience to that mandate Schweitzer went on to sketch such a life, built around the secret of the kingdom, the secret of messiahship, and the secret of the passion *(Heft 2, 1901, Das Messianitäts- und Leidensgeheimnis).*

Looking forward from the upper room, Schweitzer stresses the historical fact that the first Christian community *did* gather in historical celebration, command or not. The community did this of necessity, in a celebration that can only be called "something mysterious" *(etwas Geheimnisvolles;* the term is related to the "mystery-secrets" of Jesus), "where the individual enters into a special holy relationship with the celebrating fellowship and the personality *(Persönlichkeit)* of our Lord" (p. xi; below, p. 51). It was only in later writings, especially that on Paul in 1930, that Schweitzer got back to recounting the story of the development of the *Abendmahl* in primitive Christianity, but the plan to do so was already clear in his own mind at this time.

Beyond early Christianity, Schweitzer was sure, and said so in 1901 (pp. x-xi; below, pp. 50-51), that, in spite of all the later developments and misunderstandings about the holy communion, "our Lord's Supper is authorized, imperative, and necessary," based on the actual celebration of the early community. But he saw no profit in wranglings about "This *is.* . .," "This *means.* . .," transubstantiation, or symbolic interpretation of the words of institution. Far beyond Reformation controversies, Lutheran, Zwinglian, Calvinist, or Roman Catholic dogma—since all these center on the wrong theme, the "figurative sayings" or comparisons, "This is my body/blood"—Schweitzer saw, in progress through historical knowledge, a new—his own—solution beckoning to the historical-Jesus problem which had baffled scholarship for over a century, and to the Lord's Supper controversy that had racked Christianity for most of its nineteen-hundred-year history. No mean or modest program for a twenty-five year-old! There was, incidentally, something of a pastoral concern in all this, voiced by the *Vikar* of the St. Nicholas Church: he wanted, he wrote, to face up to such "dangerous questions" before they disturbed public opinion (p. ix; below, p. 50; Grässer, p. 38, stresses this practical concern about "disquietude" in congregations).

Schweitzer committed himself in 1901 to the rapid publication of three volumes *(Hefte)*. It is with the first volume that we deal here, made up as it is of two parts. Volume 2, its companion, also came out in 1901, and was translated into English in 1914 (see the bibliography for full details of these publications; the 1914 translation got lost in the events of World War I). The promised volume 3 (referred to in Schweitzer's preface below, at the end, p. 52) was never published, even though in 1901 it was promised "at the earliest opportunity." There was an overall title to the project on the *Abendmahl.*

Schweitzer's Plan and Publications

"The Lord's Supper *(Abendmahl)* in connection with the life of Jesus and the history of primitive Christianity"

Heft 1. *Das Abendmahlsproblem* . . . (1901)

Translated below for the first time

Erster Teil: Part I

The Problem of the Lord's Supper according to the Scholarly Research of the Nineteenth Century

(Cf. Schweitzer's thesis for the licentiate degree, *Kritische Darstellung unterschiedlicher . . . Abendmahlsauffassungen,* 1900, published 1901.)

Zweiter Teil: Part 2

The Problem of the Lord's Supper according to the Historical Accounts

Heft 2. *Das Messianitäts- und Leidensgeheimnis: Eine Skizze des Lebens Jesu* (1901)

Translated by Walter Lowrie as *The Mystery of the Kingdom: The Secret of Jesus' Messiahship and Passion* (1914)

Heft 3. *Das Abendmahl in der urchristlichen und in der altchristlichen Epochen* (proposed)

"The Lord's Supper in the primitive Christian and in the early Christian Periods."

It will be seen from this outline how in Schweitzer's proposal the *Abendmahl* both encompasses and provides the springboard for Schweitzer's work on Jesus.

Carrying Through on Jesus and Paul

In the 1903-1904 winter semester Schweitzer lectured at Strassburg on "Baptism and Lord's Supper in the New Testament and in the first four centuries," his third course given in the theology faculty. He repeated the topic in 1906-1907 and 1909-1910 (cut to "the first two centuries"). This may be taken as evidence of interest in—and work upon—the subject of volume 3. But no publication ensued, and even the lecture manuscript seems to have disappeared without trace (cf. Reumann, p. 480 and n. 34). Why? Was it never completed? Possibly the press of his many activities (plus the principalship at the theological college, summer 1901 and 1903-1906), especially the medical studies from 1905 on, prevented this. But Schweitzer himself, in his later memoirs, gave another reason:

> The third volume . . . was indeed completed and delivered in lectures, as was also the companion study on . . . Baptism, . . . Neither work was printed, however, because *The Quest of Historical Jesus,* . . . a bulky volume, . . . prevented me from getting them ready for the press.

Then came the book on Bach, medical studies, a work on the history of Pauline studies (1911) which he deemed more urgent, then Africa. His plan to "bring to its final form" the volume on the Lord's Supper and Baptism during his first furlough "was ruined by the war" and internment. As of 1930, after his philosophy-of-civilization volume (1923), Schweitzer could only say that the promised third volume

> has remained in the condition of manuscript for lectures. Whether I shall still find time and strength to complete it for the press, I know not. The thoughts which underlie it are put forth in my book, *The Mysticism of Paul the Apostle* [1930, German] *(Out of My Life and Thought,* pp. 46-47).

Schweitzer never did ready it for publication, and his only other major biblical work was the one posthumously published in 1967 on the kingdom of God. With these titles, we have noted Albert Schweitzer's total, considerable output on the New Testament.

His brief retrospective comments may, however, be amplified by noting that his 1901 *Heft* on the *Abendmahl* and Jesus did not attract the interest for which he had hoped with his new "discoveries." Reviews were limited and critical (cf. Grässer, p. 56, 62; Kümmel, pp. 328-39; Seaver, pp. 197-205). With this point must be coupled the fact that students, likely around 1902, told Schweitzer that in a course by the luckless Professor Spitta they had learned "practically nothing about previous investigations into the subject." With the approval of his mentor, Prof. Dr. H. J. Holtzmann, Schweitzer began research into the topic and became "absolutely absorbed in it," beginning with H. S. Reimarus' clandestine manuscripts in eighteenth-century Hamburg, down to his own day *(Out of My Life and Thought*, pp. 55-56). Schweitzer lectured on scientific life-of-Jesus study beginning in 1905, at first starting with Strauss, later from Reimarus to the present.

To these two facts we must add a third, on which Schweitzer (ibid., pp. 57-58) makes passing comment. In 1901 the liberal scholar at Breslau, William Wrede, had published a book on *The Messianic Secret* in the gospels. Indeed it appeared on the same day as Schweitzer's volume on "The Messianic. . . Secret." Wrede's book, in denying that Jesus as teacher entertained eschatological ideas or cherished notions of himself as messiah, cut at the heart of Schweitzer's view of Jesus in the upper room and throughout his previous ministry. And Wrede's volume elicited considerable interest and (in Germany) support. So it was that Schweitzer conceived a plan to recount the history of *Leben-Jesu-Forschung* "From Reimarus to Wrede," as he titled the book, showing how certain crucial choices by scholars of the past led inevitably to an emphasis on Mark's gospel and eschatology. His chapter on Wrede (1906 edition, chapter 19; translation, pp. 330-97) gave him the opportunity to juxtapose his own "Sketch" of a life with Wrede's book and dramatically pose the alternative (after the two of them together had knocked out the Jesus of liberal theology): *either* "thoroughgoing skepticism" about Jesus as messiah (so Wrede) *or* "thoroughgoing eschatology" as the way to interpret him as the messiah (so Schweitzer).

It would be easy to become sidetracked in the many important aspects of Schweitzer's work on "the quest." That seems to be exactly what happened with his own publication plans for volume 3 about the Lord's Supper: it was sidetracked in defending his view of the historical Jesus, by recounting the history of scholarship. Much of Schweitzer's energy just before he left for Africa went into producing a revised edition on the quest, now titled "History of Life-of-Jesus Research" (1913). The slim volume published also in 1913 on the sanity of the eschatological Jesus was a necessary bypath for his M.D. degree, but also served to defend the Jesus he had set forth.

Schweitzer's aforementioned "History of Pauline Research from the Reformation to the Present" (1911) can be described as part of a similar plan related to Paul and, indirectly, to the history of the sacraments. Along with *Paul and His Interpreters*, as this volume is known in English, Schweitzer planned a constructive volume on Paul, which was already laid out in 1911 (*Paul*, pp. ix-xi; *Out of My Life and Thought*, pp. 141-50, says he was "within a few weeks" of having it ready for the press when he had to leave for Africa). It would, of course, be an eschatological Paul. As it was, *The Mysticism of Paul the Apostle* did not see the light of day in published form for nineteen years. It is the best account of what volume 3 might have contained, at least in Paul, on the Lord's Supper.

One might chart Schweitzer's work on the *Abendmahl* within his total career thus:

1894   "Eschatological clue" about Jesus.

1897   Schleiermacher: no command to repeat in the words of institution?

Schweitzer formulates a new solution on the last / Lord's Supper and Jesus' secret.

Four years study on the history of the Lord's Supper, "all epochs."

1900   Licentiate thesis:

"Concepts of the Lord's Supper" = *Heft* 1, Part 1;
The New Testament Texts on it = *Heft* 1, Part 2.

1901   For *Habilitationsschrift*: "Messianic- and Passion-Secret" = *Heft* 2.

Published as *Das Abendmahlsproblem*, the same day as Wrede's *Messiasgeheimnis*.

1902-05   Though Schweitzer lectures on the Lord's Supper, *Heft* 3 is delayed in publication by his *Leben-Jesu* research.

1905   *Von Reimarus zu Wrede (The Quest . . .).*

1911   *Paul and His Interpreters.*

1912   *Geschichte der Leben-Jesu Forschung* (new Foreword, 1950).   *The Mysticism of Paul the Apostle* (1930).

The Kingdom of God and Primitive Christianity (written 1950-1951; published 1967).

What was central in Schweitzer's work on the New Testament over these years? Was the *Abendmahl*-problem Schweitzer's comprehensive theme? Or was it the life of Jesus? Or eschatology? See Part III, below.

II. The Contents of Schweitzer's 1901 Volume 1

It was in the personal and professional setting just sketched that Albert Schweitzer produced his volume on *das Abendmahlsproblem* in 1901. Its 62 pages, plus preface, were intended to be an opening salvo leading to a new view of the origin of the sacrament. It was to be followed immediately by a somewhat longer "sketch" of Jesus' life as Schweitzer had come to view certain parts of it in a new perspective— *Heft* 2, which appeared simultaneously; to be followed soon after a third volume on the Lord's Supper in the early church, developing Schweitzer's fuller views.

It is not unfair to place great weight on these volumes of 1901: that which follows below in translation was Schweitzer's first work in print on the New Testament, and there would be no further publication until the big book on *Leben-Jesu* research in 1906. Unlike aspiring young scholars today and many in his own time, Albert Schweitzer seems never to have published an article in a learned journal on the New Testament and never did a book review. An occasional series on the gospels in a church paper was his sole other published biblical work in this period. His books carried the burden of his claim and reputation.

This probably is the place also to record a surprising impression: that Schweitzer's books seldom go into detailed exegetical defense of his positions even on highly controverted verses like Matthew 10:23. This observation holds true for all his extant writing. The secondary literature is cited chiefly in his surveys of past scholarship. There are almost no footnotes. He gives the appearance of basing his arguments on the Greek New Testament, but seldom are the options tested as scholars are accustomed to do. Grässer (p. 54) remarks that even in his dissertation for academic advancement Schweitzer seems to write as if he were still equipped only with a Nestle text (the critical edition of the Greek New Testament) as on army maneuvers in 1894!

Hence the comment that nowhere else is Schweitzer so exegetically detailed as in Part II of the publication which follows. Readers may wish to compare the depth of the exegesis here with that of, say, Wrede, or Wellhausen on the gospels in the same period. In the medical dissertation on Jesus' psychiatric health one probably will find the Schweitzerian examples of exegesis which most rival in exactitude the pages below (pp. 45-56; below, pp. 115-29).

Since something about Schweitzer's aims in the volume has already been summarized (above, pp. 10-11), and since the English reader can for himself/herself now work through Schweitzer in the author's own original sequence—forewarned that the German is not easy to translate or the argument, especially in Part I, always simple to follow—we propose here to treat first his conclusion about the *Abendmahl* and Jesus and with it the exegetical arguments in Part II; and then to survey briefly his history of concepts from the sixteenth to the twentieth centuries. This is, after all, the way Schweitzer claims to have arrived at his findings: the broad strokes of his outline, the new interpretation of the last supper and of Jesus, were clear to him by 1898; only in 1899-1900 did he work through the newer concepts of the scholars especially in the nineteenth century (above pp. 10). Besides, as we shall ask later, is not Schweitzer a writer who, in his analysis of past scholarship, must be assessed in light of where he is moving in his survey of it? (See III, below.)

The Results

Schweitzer reached the conclusion (pp. 56-62; below, pp. 131-37) from his research that the Marcan account (14:22-25) alone preserves the authentic report of what took place in the upper room. All other accounts show the trend in the early church toward paralleling more precisely what was said over the cup and what had been said over the bread. Acceptance of Mark's version as historically authentic means (a) that there was no command from Jesus to repeat any rite, and that (b) he spoke the words "This is my body" *while* they were eating and the words "This is my blood" *after* they had all drunk of the cup, in neither case *before*.

The key to the scene, therefore, lies not in "figurative sayings" about body and blood but in "the solemn proceedings" *(feierlicher Vorgang)*; not even in some explanation of the figurative sayings on the basis of the breaking of the bread or the pouring out of the wine, but rather from the fact that Jesus in his words alluded to the secret of his passion *and* by the climactic saying in 14:25 spoke of imminent reunion with his disciples after his death in the kingdom of God. This latter verse with its highly eschatological outlook is what Schweitzer complained most treatments overlooked. Thus Jesus' suffering and eschatological expectation are inseparably combined. Jesus acts as messiah about to suffer. He at that moment knew himself to be the messiah, and he knew the eschatological secret of the passion.

These observations gave the lines of direction, of course, along which a new—and to Schweitzer, correct—life of Jesus, as messiah, intensely eschatological, would be developed. Space does not permit delineating here the Jesus whom he sketched. But some amplification of his view of Jesus in the upper room is given in the 1901 companion volume, *The Mystery of the Kingdom of God* (pp. 103-106). There Schweitzer interprets the last supper through the feeding by the seashore in Mark 6:32-44 (which for him was no miracle story but a cultic meal); both of them celebrate foretastes of the eschatological "messianic banquet" to come. *The Quest of the Historical Jesus* adds but little in dealing with these meals (pp. 376-77, 380); both are "eschatological" and "sacramental." His one page of remarks in *Out of My Life and Thought* (p. 48) may be the most clear and succinct summary. Here Schweitzer pointedly says, "What constituted the celebration, then, was not Jesus' words of institution . . ., but the prayers of thanksgiving over the bread and wine." These prayers of thanksgiving are what could convey the eschatological emphasis. We may wish to object that prayer is reported in Mark 14:22 and 23 only by two participles, "having blessed [God]" and "having given thanks [to God]," and that Schweitzer has not particularly discussed the details (cf. p. 48; below, p. 119), and that the prayer references there may simply be to a typical Jewish *berakah* and not "eschatological" at all, and that Schweitzer's assertion concerning the seaside meal that "in the prayer he gave thanks not only for the food, but also for the coming kingdom" (*Quest*, p. 376) seems read into the text—but then exegesis is not the strong suit of this bold proposal.

The Exegesis and Assumptions

How did Schweitzer arrive exegetically at the authenticity of Mark? There are two or three unstated premises which he shared with probably most New Testament scholars of his day, at least in Germany—and few others elsewhere mattered. One was the decision in nineteenth-century gospel studies that for reconstructing the life of Jesus the Fourth Gospel could safely be set aside, as a theological interpretation. A second was, having said "the Synoptics, not John," that among the first three gospels Mark had priority. Schweitzer's teacher, H. J. Holtzmann, was understood to have established that securely. Schweitzer documents the rise of such almost universal presuppositions among Protestant scholars on the continent in his *Quest* (cf. pp. 121-36, 202-205, e.g.), and he himself accepted and operated with Mark as basic source for a historical "life", though he wove in Matthean (usually M, not Q) material as of equal value (cf. *Out of My Life and Thought*, pp. 17-20, the discovery of the "eschatological clue").

In Part II, on the New Testament, Schweitzer actually begins, as one ought, with textual criticism. In Luke 22 he decides against the "Western text" (Manuscript D or Beza and its Old Latin allies), in favor of the longer reading which includes verses 19b and 20. While this may differ from what the RSV offers, it is the more preferred view today (cf. E. Schweizer, *The Lord's Supper*, pp. 18-20; or Bruce M. Metzger, *A Textual Commentary on the Greek New Testament* [New York: United Bible Societies, 1971], pp. 173-77. "C" level of certainty in the United Bible Societies Greek New Testament). Schweitzer's other textual observations show how later manuscripts tended to assimilate all four accounts in Mark, Matthew, Luke, and Paul and to make them alike. But only as differences stand out can we recover an original. The Textus Receptus in Greek and the King James Version in English reflect the long centuries of textual harmonization. If one wonders why Schweitzer includes the text from Justin Martyr's *Apology* (1.66.3), it is because the version there had developed to a perfect symmetry:

Do this in remembrance of me. This is my body.

This is my blood.

Gone from Justin's account are all references to blood "poured out," "my body '(given) for you'," the phrase "for many," the covenant, and so forth (see below, pp. 128-29).

When characterizing Mark, Schweitzer puts his emphasis on the often unobserved differences from the other accounts, indeed on Mark's peculiarities. Likely Schleiermacher's observation on the absence of a command to repeat the rite set Schweitzer thinking in this direction. He quotes (pp. 48-49; below, p. 119-20) the radical critic Bruno Bauer (see Part I, pp. 12-13; below, pp. 75-76) as the first to record that Mark presents as narrative what others present as a command from Jesus:

Mark 14:23-24	*Matthew 26:27-28*
And having taken a cup, having given thanks, he gave (it) to them, *and they all drank from it. And he said to them,* "This is my blood. . . ."	And having taken a cup, having given thanks, he gave (it) to them *saying "Drink from it, all of you.* For this is my blood. . . ."

Bauer objected that it would be "fantasy" for a man sitting there physically and personally to think of offering his body and blood to others—something brought home to Schweitzer when watching the Passion Play at Oberammergau in 1900 (cf. pp. 41-42, below, p. 109; *Out of My Life and Thought*, p. 43; how absurd for twelve men to sit with bits of bread in their hand or a cup poised, waiting for Jesus to say the interpretative words!); others have objected to any thought of drinking "blood" in a Jewish setting. But Bauer missed the eschatological saying in 14:25. Schweitzer put these points together. When one finds the "figurative saying" *after* the drinking of the cup and views the *eschatological* hope of reunion soon at the messianic feast after Jesus' death, then it all makes sense. Mark is saying something different from all other accounts.

Now, in his next to the last sentence on the peculiarity of the Marcan account, Schweitzer interjects what may be called another premise of his approach, the use of the "either/or." He writes (p. 50; below, p. 120-21, italics added): in Mark we have before us *"either . . .* an absolutely incomprehensible portrayal . . . *or* the authentic account with which the investigation must begin" into the *Abendmahlsproblem*. It has been well documented (by James M. Robinson in his 1968 introduction to *The Quest*, pp. xii, xiv, xvi, xvii) that Schweitzer loved to pick out "Either-Or decisions" as decisive in the history of research. He did this in his 1906 book by highlighting from the nineteenth century the questions "either purely historical or purely supernatural" (which Strauss transcended with his "mythical interpretation"); "either Synoptic or Johannine," "either eschatological or uneschatological," and "either Mark as a whole must be recognized as historical or one must be quite skeptical" like Bauer—or Wrede. (Each of the last three options Schweitzer found answered by the former of the two choices.) We may now add an earlier example of this fourth "either-or" in Schweitzer's work: in 1901 he answered, as he would increasingly, that either Mark is authentic or his account is fantasy, and there is no other solution with regard to Jesus in the upper room.

Schweitzer's comparison of the other accounts (pp. 50-55; below, pp. 123-29) is then devoted to showing how, in deviating from Mark, each tends to make the bread and cup actions more and more parallel, Matthew slightly, Paul in 1 Corinthians 11 more so, Luke still more, and Justin perfectly. In the case of Luke's long text, Schweitzer even points out *two* eschatological sayings, verses 15-16 and verse 18, both of them before bread and (second) cup associated with the "figurative sayings"; thus the eschatological reference stands over the entire meal. But this is a literary construction, aesthetic, liturgical. Schweitzer's argument for Marcan authenticity (pp. 56-60, below, pp. 131-34) amounts to a reprise of what we have already noted: Mark's account "in no way" reflects the "congregational celebration" in the early church, with its trend toward parallelism and harmonization. Mark's is, we might say, the "only ball game in town"; it is "authentic or meaningless" (p. 60; below, p. 134).

The Historical Survey

Knowing what he was aiming at, we may now ask how Schweitzer presented and measured the massive scholarly research of the nineteenth century (actually from the sixteenth century until 1899) which he surveyed in Part I of his book. If he is correct in stating that his theory was in mind by 1898, then his examination of the secondary literature from Zwingli to Harnack and other contemporaries was done with his emerging view of Jesus and the supper as a guide.

We shall not again note his preface (cf. above, pp. 7, 9-12) except to call attention to his avowed aim. It was, he writes (p. viii, below p. 49) more than "the advancement of a new historical conception of the last/Lord's Supper" *(Abendmahlsauffassung)*. There is "the practical purpose of setting forth *(abgeben)* the historical *(historisch)* foundation of our modern celebration of the Lord's Supper and of historically *(geschichtlich)* justifying our present practice," as it is rendered below. It would be a neat solution if one could claim that Schweitzer was here contrasting *"historisch"* and *"geschichtlich"* in the way Martin Kähler was in this period, as, respectively, "past historical" or "objective history" and "historic" or "existential, meaningful-for-me history." But Schweitzer seems to use the terms otherwise just a few pages later: "Our celebration is not based on the historical *(geschichtlich)* tradition . . . but directly on the historical *(historisch)* celebration" (p. x; below,

p. 51). And later, therefore, "we must believe in history *(die Geschichte),*" for faith is bound up with "the progress of historical *(geschichtlich)* knowledge" (p. xi, below, p. 52). Part of the solution is that he found in the "history of Jesus" a "dogmatic history," that is, "history as moulded by theological beliefs"—in a word, eschatology (*Quest*, p. 351). In any case, Schweitzer meant to find in Mark a historical account in every sense of the word, for it tells what happened when one who regarded himself as messiah gave thanks, broke and gave bread, and so forth, just as it also provides Jesus' eschatological vision of reunion later on with his disciples.

In a sense, all Schweitzer needed to prove was that no view of the supper put forth in nineteenth-century research was adequate to explain both what Jesus said and did in the upper room and what developed in the early Christian community. That was a conclusion to which he had come as a student in 1897-1898: "I came to realize how exceedingly unsatisfactory were the current explanations of the significance of the historical ceremony which Jesus celebrated with His disciples, and of the origin of the primitive Christian ceremony of the Supper" (*Out of My Life and Thought*, p. 25). To document such an inadequacy of existing theories would open the way for his "new way" of approach (p. 40; below, p. 108), his new solution, and ultimately "a new life of Jesus" (p. 62; below, p. 137). But Schweitzer, as usual, sought in the process of his historical survey to do even more. By the very way he posed the problem (Part I, chapter IX and throughout), he could indicate the tensions within the total concept which had to be bridged by his eschatological link.

One way of doing this was through the typology or classification he used for organizing the multitude of views on the supper over a 370-year period. Schweitzer found two main streams (p. 5; below, p. 61, for which he employed terms which need some explaining, no matter what the English rendering:

A. There is first the *Darstellungsmoment*, rendered in the translation below as "moment of presentation," though it could also suggest "impulse, impetus, factor" of "representation" or "depiction." When Brilioth used the term, his translator employed "Memorial-aspect." What Schweitzer means by it are "the actions and words of Jesus during the historical celebration" in the upper room. That would involve the emphasis on his praying, breaking bread, taking wine, giving these to the disciples, and saying "This is my body/blood. . . ."

B. The other is the *Genussmoment*, translated below as "moment of partaking" or "factor, impulse, impetus" of "reception." The Brilioth translator, A. G. Hebert, speaks of the "emphasis on the reception of the bread and wine in the act of communion." Schweitzer defines it as "the meaning of the participants' eating and drinking, as it is to result from the essence of the celebration."

Schweitzer then combines these two poles of emphasis in four possible ways, recognizing degrees of stress on each when they are combined. Naturally a translator must use an agreed phrase to make Schweitzer's four combinations at all manageable in English. The four—which Schweitzer saw as unfolding chronologically from the Reformation to his day—together with examples of each are outlined as follows:

(1) Emphasis on the *Darstellungsmoment.* A one-sided stress on the moment of presentation, especially the "words of institution" or "figurative statements" was to be found in all traditional interpretations of the Lord's Supper, Catholic, Lutheran, and Reformed, even if the first two held to a "crass, realistic" sense and the Reformed to a "symbolic" one (cf. p. xi; below, p. 51). Schweitzer bothers to mention only Zwingli as example (pp. 5-6; below, pp. 63-64). Most Catholic and Protestant church views of his day fitted here, however.

(2) A twofold concept, stressing *Darstellungsmoment,* but with some emphasis on "reception." Such a two-sided interpretation takes the "moment of presentation" by Jesus as basic but grants "a secondary importance" to "reception." Calvin (pp. 6-7; below, p. 64) exemplifies this, though he is allowed to have stressed both equally and, of course, took both what Jesus did with the bread and wine and the reception by the congregation as "symbolical." Calvin's view prevailed over Zwingli's and set the stage for the series of nineteenth-century examples which Schweitzer offers (chapter 3; below, pp. 65-69). Commentaries, like De Wette's (1836-1837), Keim's life of Jesus (1872), and the biblical theology of Schweitzer's teacher, H. J. Holtzmann (1897), are among the examples from which excerpts are cited.

(3) Emphasis on the *Genussmoment.* Interpretations which stress "reception" and develop in a one-sided way the "moment of partaking" begin in the early nineteenth century with David Friedrich Strauss, who is for Schweitzer one of the turning points in gospels study generally. Strauss (1836) saw the significance of Mark 14:25 and held that Jesus' own expectation was that he and his followers would

celebrate Passover the next year in the kingdom; Jesus' death intervened, and the disciples then gave both his death and the meal a new meaning, and added a command to repeat the rite. Among Schweitzer's other examples is his Strassburg colleague, Friedrich Spitta, to whom he gives high praise for emphasizing in a book of 1893 an "eschatological" interpretation. It was an anticipation of the "messianic banquet" of the Old Testament prophets (cf. Is. 25:6-8, 65:12-14, 55:1-2; Zech. 9:16-17) that Jesus offered to his disciples. But Spitta erred in finding the eschatological note only in Jesus' closing words in the upper room rather than throughout, and in equating Jesus himself as messiah with the food and drink offered. Indeed, this was the frequent error in this approach, to bring back into the picture the "figurative sayings," so that Jesus who offers the elements is identified as himself what is received. (Cf. chapters 4-5; below, pp. 71-84, especially p. 84 for Schweitzer's overall judgment.)

(4) A twofold concept, stressing *Genussmoment* but with some emphasis on "presentation." In chapter VI Schweitzer takes up examples of those who in a two-sided way take "the moment of partaking" as basic but grant "a secondary importance" to the *Darstellungsmoment*. All his illustrations come from the 1890s. One would have to say the excerpts cited are a very mixed bag, seemingly sharing only a general agreement on (3) but enough dissatisfaction with it to bring back some emphasis on (1). Harnack's remarks are *obiter dicta* in a paper on Justin Martyr (his *Dogmengeschichte* would offer far more than the one page mentioned on his views). Haupt's lecture lets eschatology fade away but explains things by Jesus' "personality" (a term which, we shall see, Schweitzer welcomed). Schultzen's work made both "moments" almost equal. R. A. Hoffmann's book actually makes the *Darstellungsmoment* even more prominent. One is tempted to ask whether we really do have here examples of the fourth category which Schweitzer had created. But readers will note in these pages that Schweitzer's real measuring rod, eschatology, is coming to the fore.

The concluding chapters of this study (VII-IX) allow Schweitzer, using one of his favorite analogies, that of a battlefield, to show how all four positions had their defenders when he wrote, around 1900. Jülicher (1892) had even put Zwingli in modern terms. But even more, Schweitzer can stress the dilemma of *all* existing views about the last supper and the Lord's Supper. When *Genussmoment* is stressed, communal meals and *Abendmahl* become identical; when *Darstel-*

lungsmoment is stressed, the two become utterly separated (pp. 29-30; below pp. 94-95). To explain the early Christian celebration, the way Spitta does, as a joyous "messianic-foretaste" meal, does justice to it but at the expense of the "historical celebration" by Jesus in the upper room; to concentrate on *Darstellungsmoment* may satisfy for the upper room, but does not explain early church practice (pp. 30-31; below, pp. 95-96). One must speak of a "contradiction" here (*Antinomie*; Chap. VIII, Section 3; cf. p. ix, below, p. 50), indeed an antinomy that is insoluble. Not to find a link between Jesus and the sacrament leads to skepticism and becomes a dangerous question in the public mind and for the church. But Schweitzer, "in a practical, edifying, and conciliatory spirit" (p. xi, below p. 52) is ready with his new solution—eschatology.

III. Assessing Schweitzer's Achievements

Volume 1 of Schweitzer's proposed trilogy on the *Abendmahl* in connection with the life of Jesus and the history of primitive Christianity, translated below into English for the first time, with its two parts on the history of research and on the early Christian texts about the last supper, reveals something of the flair and style that marked Schweitzer's later writings. Cumbersome though some of the sections are, we find scintillating phrases and even some of the same comparisons which are to appear in more famous books.

Thus, for example, when he compares the question of the Lord's Supper in Christian history to an intermittently active volcano, with three phases of action (pp. 1-2; below, pp. 57-58), we recognize the same famous point of comparison employed when he spoke of "justification by faith" as but a minor crater in Pauline theology compared with the central volcano of being "in Christ" (*Mysticism*, pp. 220-21, 225). When he says (p. vii; below, p. 47) that Schleiermacher's point (that in Mark Jesus gave no command to repeat the meal) served "to 'awaken us out of our dogmatic slumber,' in a Kantian sense," Schweitzer is alluding to a well-known phrase of Kant's, on whom he wrote his first dissertation. To say that thus "Schleiermacher is the Hume of the question of causality in the problem of the Lord's Supper" (p. vii; below, p. 48) is to give Schleiermacher's point the place that David Hume, the Scottish Enlightenment philosopher, had with regard to causality in connection with the miracles. When Schweitzer (p. xi; below, p. 51) comments that, for those who concentrate on the "words of institution," there can be only a symbolic (Zwinglian) or a literal interpretation (as in Luther) and that "any mediating interpretation is untenable" (literally in his German, "What is in between, is from evil"), he is echoing Matthew 5:37, "Let what you say be simply 'Yes' or 'No'; anything more than this comes from evil." There are thus flashes of Schweitzerian style, even in this licentiate dissertation. But how does this work fare in retrospect?

Methodology and Results

(1) First of all, it should be observed that in this 1901 volume we have the first occasion where Schweitzer employed his pattern of (a) presenting the history of research on a topic and then (b) providing the solution to the problem. As Grässer puts it (p. 45), from knowledge of the problem in the past, Schweitzer obtains the answer to the problem in the present.

The volume before us includes both (a) a history of research, and (b) analysis of the earliest texts to present a new solution on the *Abendmahl.* If we include *Heft* 2 on the mystery of Jesus' messiahship and passion, the solution (b) would be even more fully spelled out.

The same pattern holds for Schweitzer's work on the life of Jesus, except that the sketch of that life (Schweitzer's solution) appeared first, in 1901 (*Heft* 2), while the survey of research was published only in 1906. With Paul the history of scholarship came first, in 1911, the constructive volume on the apostle not until 1930.

Schweitzer himself tells us (*Out of My Life and Thought*, pp. 142-43) that he thus followed this "laborious byroad" of expounding the history of the problem three times, on the Lord's Supper, on Jesus, and on Paul. For these byroads he, writing some thirty years after the *Abendmahl* volume, blames Aristotle who led him to evolve this approach. He had read—cursed be the day!—in the *Metaphysics* how Aristotle developed "the problem of philosophy out of a criticism of previous philosophizing." He felt he had to do likewise, to find "scientific and artistic satisfaction" thus in his research.

But, on Schweitzer's own words in 1901, he did not need any such history of research to discern the *Abendmahlsproblem.* Schleiermacher alone had posed the problem for him. And the solution Schweitzer "was certain of, independently of modern research, already in the fall of 1897" (p. viii; below, p. 48). We may say that Schweitzer's survey of research on the Lord's Supper no doubt clarified many issues for him and certainly earned him the licentiate degree, but his testimony contemporary with the dissertation itself suggests that the byroad was not necessary for the results. With regard to *Leben-Jesu* studies, we have already suggested (p. 14 above) that Schweitzer's enormous survey *Von Reimanus zu Wrede* was written especially to defend and promote his earlier sketch of a life of Jesus. If we allow that Schweitzer, as he says (above, p. 15), was within weeks of completing his book on the mysticism of Paul in 1912, then perhaps the (a)—(b) pattern holds more for his work on Paul, even though there was hiatus of nineteen years in publishing the two volumes.

To the degrees indicated, the pattern of "history of the problem"— "solution to the problem" must therefore be qualified in the three different cases.

(2) Whether Schweitzer's surveys of past scholarship were integral to his coming to definition and solution of a problem or were in the first two instances, at least, devices to buttress his solutions otherwise (almost intuitively) arrived at, we must, since the surveys are related to the solution, raise the question of how objective his treatment was of the views of others. This question of Schweitzer's tendentiousness is not always raised, and we shall be able to pursue it here only briefly with regard to the *Abendmahlsproblem* (see further, Reumann, pp. 479-80).

We have already inquired (above, p. 24) whether any of the four examples cited really fit under category (4) in Schweitzer's typology of views on the *Abendmahl*. Indeed, the typology itself could be questioned; few experts seem to have been impressed enough by it to note it, let alone employ it further (see point (3) below). Chronologically, the four categories are presented by Schweitzer "in the order in which they made their appearance historically" (p. 5; below, p. 62), and that holds if we regard Zwingli, Calvin or De Wette, D. F. Strauss, and Harnack as, respectively, the initial protagonist of each. But were they? Would fuller research turn up earlier examples? Schweitzer calls to testify for his sequence a strange array of mostly Germans (two scholars wrote in French), from commentaries, monographs, articles, lives of Jesus, and biblical theology—but no Englishmen; no Catholics; no indication that other writers in the same genre of "lives" or biblical theology need not be consulted. The list yields a rather lopsided concentration for options (2) and (3). The figures are for category (1), two (Zwingli, Jülicher); for (2), ten; for (3), six; for (4), four.

(Schmiedel, pp. 32-34, below, pp. 98-100, seems to belong in category (1).)

If we take seriously Schweitzer's claim (p. viii; below, p. 48) that he chose to write on the nineteenth century because it "lies closest to us" but that he could have utilized any other period—presumably early Christian, medieval, or Reformation—then our response is not disbelief but puzzlement. Not disbelief, because he had worked through some of the patristic evidence for lectures at Strassburg and knew more of the Reformation than Zwingli and Calvin, at least through his 1897 examination assignment. But puzzlement: could the four categories have obtained prior to Zwingli? But what of pietists, non-German rationalism, and liberals outside Germany in the period between 1530 and 1900? What Schweitzer actually speaks of for all periods, is, literally "the same laws" at work (p. vii; below, p. 48), but his chapter on "laws which govern the connection between individual questions" (*der gesetzmässige Zusammenhang*, pp. 26-31; below, pp. 91-96) at best hints of "eschatology" as the link. How could the same picture obtain in any period but the nineteenth century, especially if everything until Zwingli was centered in Jesus' historical actions in the upper room? Finally, is not Schweitzer's measuring stick of eschatology apparent as he presents particular scholars?

We may also ask where Schweitzer's own sketch fits in his fourfold category. He nowhere gives a direct answer, but the implication is that it transcends that way of asking the question. For "eschatology" supersedes *Darstellungs-* and *Genussmomente*, or properly, they must be integrated under it. But Wilhelm Averbeck (see bibliography) treats Schweitzer under the liberals and History-of-Religions School; his massive study credits Spitta with raising the eschatological interpretation of the Supper into prominence among liturgiologists.

(3) As already suggested above (p. 27), Schweitzer's survey and pattern of research on the *Abendmahl* in the nineteenth century has left little or no impression on subsequent liturgical or even, surprisingly, New Testament scholarship. Professor Grässer (pp. 62-64) surveys a good deal of evidence, chiefly negative, to reach his conclusion that Schweitzer's "position no more plays any role in present-day discussion of the Supper" (p. 63). A few reflections can be noted in French works on the Eucharist (J. Réville, 1908; M. Goguel, 1910) and a bit more added from the Scottish scholar G. H. C. Macgregor (1928), the American Schweitzer enthusiast Walter Lowrie (1953), and recent

treatments in German such as those of W. Averbeck (1967), Hermann Patsch (1972), or Helmut Feld (1976) (details on all of these in Reumann, pp. 483-84). But the influence is surprisingly slight even when the exegetical work is included, and very scant when only the survey-of-research is considered.

A case in point is the volume by the liturgical scholar, Yngve Brilioth, *Eucharistic Faith and Practice* (Swedish 1925-1926). He specifically cites (p. 3) Schweitzer's typology and pays it the tribute that "perhaps . . . the permanent value of his survey consists chiefly in his energetic discrimination of the two types," that is, *Darstellungs-* and *Genussmoment*. But Brilioth senses that the object of Schweitzer was to show the impossibility "of all these views in order to leave a clear field for his own eschatological view." But Schweitzer, he goes on, "cannot be said to have succeeded any better than" Jülicher or the others at solving the problem of how the rite came to be repeated (p. 5). And when Brilioth does his own, much more thorough, history of past eucharistic views, he gives evidence for asking whether, for example, Zwingli's view was "merely symbolistic" (pp. 153-54) and did not strongly stress "Communion-fellowship" (= *Genussmoment?*, pp. 157-58) as well.

In modern ecumenical dialogue Schweitzer's analysis of past history of the Lord's Supper has played no part. (But see below, (9), on how his views may indirectly be reflected in liturgical developments.)

New Testament Findings

If Schweitzer in his books of 1901 set for himself a pattern of research and solution, in part tendentious, which however had little influence in subsequent liturgical-historical scholarship on the Lord's Supper, what of the area of New Testament analysis (Part II in the translation below), where his reputation would lead us to expect greater effects? We already have both paid tribute to the depth of exegesis (for Schweitzer's published works) here but cautioned about its lack of detail (above, p. 16).

(4) Schweitzer may be said to have met reasonably well his own goals set in this licentiate dissertation. Plainly committed to the use of the historical-critical method as practiced in his day (p. 2; below, p. 58), yet aware from the history of research of the mixed results and indeed skepticism to which it led (ibid.), he made it a primary aim to show that "the supper problem" is not a matter of reaching decisions

on a whole series of separate questions and then bringing together one's conclusions the best way possible, but rather of finding "the laws" which mutually condition all the individual questions (p. 3; below, p. 59). For Schweitzer, past efforts showed that "we do not have the key" to explain the connection between Jesus' historical and the early church's continuing celebrations (p. ix; below, p. 50). He himself repeatedly, therefore, sets forth his contentions that we need a total conception of Jesus, upper room, and early church, and that the new solution lies in eschatology.

As for the individual questions, Schweitzer lists some 21 at the outset of his discussion (pp. 3-4; below, pp. 59-61). They comprise a "laundry list" which arises from the exegetical literature of the day. Some of them (e.g., 1 and 2, involving the "figurative sayings") fall outside of Schweitzer's area of emphasis, once we see that the eschatological factor was his focal point (questions 17-18). Others are dealt with by his decision for the priority and historicity of Mark's account (e.g., number 20, on which text to prefer; 5 and 6, on the command to repeat; and probably 3 and 4, on chronology).

Actually Schweitzer seems not to discuss, here or elsewhere, the chronological problem *within* Mark. Mark 14:12, 14 suggests the meal in the upper room is the Passover meal; 14:1 implies it could be pre-Passover; 14:22-25 need not be read as referring to a Passover meal. While some exegetes took 14:25 as expectation that the Passover meal next year would be "in the kingdom of God," Schweitzer, without expressly saying so, must take 14:25 as referring not to the Passover but simply to the "messianic, eschatological banquet," for his famous closing words on Jesus' life both in the "Sketch" and in 1906 are that Jesus died "on the afternoon of the fourteenth of Nisan, when they ate the Paschal lamb at even"(*Mystery*, p. 173; cf. *Quest*, p. 397). That is, he follows the Johannine chronology.

Other questions, such as those on John 6 or on Paul, or the relation of the Agape and the Lord's Supper in the early church, are not dealt with in the 1901 writings. One must look to later works by Schweitzer to find his answers. (See (6) below.)

We are thus willing to agree that, in spite of gaps, Schweitzer has made his point that an overall concept is needed to treat both Jesus at the last supper and the Lord's Supper of the early church. These broader questions were in Schweitzer's mind, even if he does not address them all satisfactorily here.

(5) Several times it has been suggested that Schweitzer's overall view of "the supper," in connection with Jesus historically (at the Sea of Galilee, Mark 6:30-44, and in the upper room) and with the early church and indeed the first several centuries, must be pieced together from subsequent writings since the proposed third volume on the *Abendmahlsproblem* never was published. The best places for readers to pursue the further story in Schweitzer's works include (in English) *Mystery*, pp. 103-106, 166-67, 172; *Quest*, pp. 376-77, 380-81, cf. 396-97; *Mysticism*, pp. 227-30, 237-60; 265-83, 291-92. It is particularly in the pages of chapter XI of the last book mentioned that Schweitzer spells out what he might have said in the planned volume 3. (Cf. also *Out of My Life and Thought*, pp. 45-48, 250.)

The gist of Schweitzer's view is that Jesus took over from the Old Testament prophets the expectation of the messianic banquet of the last days. The feast-sacrament by the lake in Mark 6, which Schweitzer even calls "the first Eucharist," consecrated his followers as companions for the messianic feast of the kingdom. Jesus repeated this at the last supper in Jerusalem, adding reference to his approaching death which would be the means of bringing the kingdom.

In the early church the "words of institution" (which properly only Jesus, not an apostle or minister "playing" his role, could say) were not repeated at the meal, nor was there a command to repeat a rite. Instead, the meal was, like those by the lake and in the upper room, celebrated looking forward to the messianic feast. Mark 14:25 thus assumes the role for the disciples of "a command to repeat the meal." After Easter the disciples expected the risen Jesus to come to them as they sat at table in Jerusalem. (Here Schweitzer looks to the references in Acts 1-2 and denies that the promise that Jesus would lead the disciples into Galilee, Mark 14:28, was fulfilled. But, on analogy with Matthew 10:23, would this not then be an unfulfilled prophecy on the lips of Jesus which must be genuine?) Thus there arose, out of eschatological expectancy, the repetition in Jerusalem of the last supper. Thus, for the earliest church Schweitzer posited only such thanksgiving meals built around the return of Jesus, no "services of the word" without a meal-fellowship in this period.

Paul took over this eschatological sacrament from primitive Christianity. His Lord's Supper was the church's thanksgiving meal, but his account makes Jesus enjoin the command to repeat (1 Cor. 11:23, 25) and to that extent missed the point of Mark 14:25. While maintaining the biblical view that unethical conduct can make the sacrament invalid (1 Cor. 10, 11), Paul also interpreted it on the basis of what Schweitzer saw as central in Paul: the mystical "being 'in Christ'." Bread and wine bring fellowship with Christ's body and blood. It was Paul, according to Schweitzer, who thus opened the way for the sacrament to develop from a "meal-celebration" to a "distribution-celebration" as eschatological expectation died out.

It is in the Fourth Gospel and Ignatius, however, that bread and wine are taken to become Christ's flesh and blood (John 6:53-56). Future union, envisioned in the earliest view of the meal, had become in Paul a present union, and now the eschatological aspect was lost completely. The elements became "medicine of immortality" (Ignatius, *Ephesians* 20). From Ignatius and Justin down to 1900 the "eschatological sacrament conception" was lost—without which one cannot even think through the history of the sacrament properly.

So Schweitzer contends, in his book on *The Mysticism of Paul* (cf. Grässer, p. 59, n. 3). More succinct in his statement, indeed somewhat different, in *Out of My Life and Thought* (p. 48): in the upper room "what constituted the celebration, then, was . . . the prayers of thanksgiving over the bread and wine"; these prayers also gave meaning to the meals of the early church, pointing forward to the expected messianic meal. (Schweitzer assumed that, like the Lord's Prayer, these prayed for the coming of the kingdom.) Hence, indeed, comes the name "Eucharist," that is, (prayers of) "thanksgiving" for Jesus' return at the future kingdom.

One may lament that so many questions remain, which volume 3 might have answered.

(6) Schweitzer's New Testament findings in the volume before us (Part II below) have by no means received the general endorsement of subsequent biblical scholarship. There is probably less agreement with him here than on his controverted view of Jesus, where Schweitzer's messianic figure has proven completely out of step not only with the Bultmannian view of a non-messianic teacher but also with the Jesus of the "New Quest" (e.g., G. Bornkamm). Even conservative scholars who accept that Jesus did regard himself as messiah, though they would welcome Schweitzer's handling of Mark as firm history, would not agree on its corollary, namely, the repudiation of so much in other gospels as later development. What stands out as Schweitzer's supreme achievement regarding Jesus is, of course, the recovery of eschatology,

so that no one since his time dare overlook the issue. But even there Schweitzer's work is for moderns limited by the fact that Johannes Weiss had earlier underscored it for Jesus' preaching on the kingdom, and by the fact one must ask always, What kind of eschatology? Schweitzer's apocalyptically dogmatic Jesus has by no means carried the day.

Space limits our comments here to one or two salient points in Schweitzer's treatment of the last supper texts. We have already agreed that Schweitzer was right in preferring the longer text of Luke, including 22:19b-20. The priority of Mark, however, is at least as disputed today as it was in Schweitzer's day, and many would not follow him in seeing Mark 14:22-25 as the earliest account we possess—certainly not as it stands, without recognizing source and redaction, emphatically not as *either* history *or* fantasy. Recent scholarship views *all accounts,* Mark's included, as reflecting the interests of the early church. "The eschatological perspective" of Mark 14:25 which Schweitzer stressed must be recognized today as *one* of the theological motifs at work in the passages, but the death of Jesus and the covenant loom important too. To Schweitzer's horror, it *could* be that Mark 14:25 has its origin in the Lucan account (so Schürmann); and the Pauline account (with Jesus' death prominent) is judged by many to be more likely genuine than the Lucan one with its eschatology. (All these views are documented in Eduard Schweizer's *RGG* article.)

Opinions vary, and fluctuate, but it must be said that Albert Schweitzer's New Testament exegesis did not convince the experts and solve things as he had hoped. When measured by subsequent scholarship, it becomes but an interesing example of pre-form critical judgments, indeed naive on source criticism. (Cf. further, Reumann, pp. 484-85, on Schweitzer's contributions here.)

(7) In passing, we may pose the question of whether *Abendmahl* was Schweitzer's central theme out of which his life-of-Jesus studies emerged (Reumann); or whether a new concept of the life of Jesus was his driving passion from student days on, in which study of the *Abendmahl* was but a starting point for his thesis (Groos; Picht, pp. 46-47; and Grässer, p. 39). While the usual view is that a *Leben-Jesu* was Schweitzer's overarching concern, note the umbrella topic for his proposed three volumes, namely, *das Abendmahlsproblem,* and the fact that one would not come to Schweitzer's view of Jesus without the upper room and the sacramental meal by the lake. What Schweitzer

specifically added under "eschatology" to Weiss's correct location there of Jesus' preaching about the kingdom was not only Jesus' ministry in general but specifically his view of the messianic banquet and of the meals during the ministry. Even if interest in the Lord's Supper dropped out of Schweitzer's later writing schedule, it stands as the integrating factor for his work around 1900 and helps achieve an overall unity to it. (For further discussion, see Reumann, pp. 481-83.)

Practical and Ecumenical Results

(8) On the practical level, Schweitzer saw no need for the church of his day to give up celebrating the Lord's Supper in spite of the grave questions posed (cf. pp. vii-ix; below, pp. 48-50). Though no answers were forthcoming from other theories, ecclesiastical or scholarly, about the link between Jesus and the church's meal, and though Schleiermacher's appeal to canonical authority no longer sufficed in Schweitzer's day (pp. v-vi, ix-x; below, pp. 46, 49-51), Schweitzer felt he had found a solution in eschatology, historically grounded in sure New Testament texts. And he had great faith in *Geschichte* and the ability of historical-critical scholarship to recover the truth (p. xi; below, pp. 51-52; cf. Grässer, p. 42). As a pastor at St. Nicholas Church, therefore, he kept the practice of the Lord's Supper undisturbed (Grässer, p. 61).

In another sense, though, he should have changed it drastically, for Schweitzer also had bold words about reform of the Lord's Supper. A paragraph in *The Mysticism of Paul* calls for thinking "our own thoughts," in the face of changed world conditions, "about the redemptive significance of the death of Jesus and all that is connected with it," based now on the "original primitive-Christian doctrines." We cannot simply take over the primitive-Christian sort of eschatology, of course, but must recast the traditional material "by a creative act of the Spirit" (or is it, "the spirit"?), as Ignatius and Justin did, indeed as Paul had (for example, in linking ethics with the personality of Christ) (p. 291, cf. pp. 283, 286, 333). Grässer (p. 60) calls attention to a phrase not included on p. 333 of the English, about attaining to "an idea (!) of supratemporal validity by the deepest thinking through of what is temporally conditioned" (German, p. 323).

What that kind of program would have implied, Schweitzer never spells out. The depth of his concern may have escaped notice, Grässer suggests (p. 61), because (1) as Schweitzer said in a note to George Seaver (and reported in the latter's biography of Schweitzer, p. 197, n.

1) he never debated the problem with his critics but simply laid out the problem; and (2) he felt eschatology by its nature has an impulse for ethics. Therefore in ethics lies the personal component of the eschatological solution. Indeed, Jesus likely used eschatological materials regarding the imminence of the kingdom and the messianic banquet to gain a hearing for the ethical. Would his reform have moved in such an ethical direction—an ethicizing sacrament?

Or would it have been development in light of "Jesus' personality," that elemental factor which Schweitzer in 1901 found so basic in the historical figure? As he put it, "Our faith is built upon the personality of Jesus. . . . Theology . . . is free . . . to found our Christian view . . . solely upon the personality of Jesus Christ, irrespective of the form in which it expressed itself in his time. He has destroyed this form with his death. History prompts theology"—and prompts liturgy for the Lord's Supper, we may add—"to this unhistorical step"(*Mystery*, pp. 157-59).

Schweitzer's musings, if that is what they were, about the Lord's Supper in Christendom, boldly reconceived according to its essence in primitive Christian eschatology, would of course transcend old splits between Reformation parties like the Lutherans and Reformed. It is not impossible that he further conceived of an "ecumenical" solution based on his work which would have beckoned to Roman Catholics also, when one recalls a passage in his *Memoirs of Childhood and Youth* (German, 1924). He remembers there with fondness how his father's Protestant Church in Günsbach was shared with the Catholics by edict of Louis XIV, so that the Catholic congregation had the choir for mass. That "Protestant-Catholic" church building was for Schweitzer a symbol of the fact that confessional differences would one day vanish and was a prophecy and an exhortation toward a religious future where all true Christians would unite (p. 68). Could not a sacramental understanding which replaced old differences show the way?

(9) We conclude with a paradox. Schweitzer's work on the Lord's Supper has left little mark from its survey of research, none in practical worship life in Strassburg or elsewhere, and had a mixed reception at best in the history of interpretation of the Lord's Supper texts. Yet what he emphasized—the church's meal as an eschatological feast, a foretaste of one to come in the kingdom; the mood of "holy hilarity," as in Acts 1-2; de-emphasis of the cross and death of Jesus, of confession of sins, and Good-Friday piety, and even of the words of institution, which have been replaced by, or incorporated into, a "eucharistic prayer"—all that

has simply become commonplace in much recent liturgy-making, post-Vatican II Roman Catholic, Anglican, Lutheran, even Presbyterian-Reformed and Free Church. How did that come about?

One suspects the links are only indirect. Schweitzer is known for bringing eschatology front and center in New Testament studies, and thus into theology generally, and hence into the ecumenical movement (cf. the World Council of Churches' theme at Evanston, in 1954, "Christ—the Hope of the World"). But his work on the Lord's Supper is not widely known. Yet enough of his isolated statements have been quoted by liturgiologists to make one suspect an influence which deserves further study. For example, Luther D. Reed (American Lutheran, active in Faith and Order) quoted Schweitzer (as others have quoted Oscar Cullmann) in favor of the exclusive centrality of the Lord's Supper from the outset in Christian worship: "All the praying, prophesying, preaching, and teaching took place within the framework of the thanksgiving at the celebration of the Lord's Supper" (*The Lutheran Liturgy* [Philadelphia: Muhlenberg Press, 1947], p. 234, rev. ed. p. 245; cf. *Mysticism*, p. 253). What we have already quoted (p. 32, above) about the "prayers of thanksgiving" as constitutive for the celebration with Jesus and in the early church sounds like a set principle in liturgical reform in the 1960s and 1970s (though Schweitzer's context was scarcely preserved); the Lord's Supper has become "the Great Thanksgiving."

That Schweitzer's impact is derived, and not direct, is well suggested by the book *Eucharist and Eschatology*, by Geoffrey Wain-wright. Spurred by a call from within the Faith and Order movement for a study of the Eucharist in eschatological perspective, Wainwright begins his account with how, around the turn of the century, New Testament scholars rediscovered the "eschatological dimension of the gospel." Schweitzer's name receives pride of place (pp. 7-8, 11), but only for his books beginning with *The Mystery of the Kingdom of God* (p. 155, n. 6). Schweitzer's germinal work, translated below, is unmentioned, and seemingly unknown. Here, as elsewhere so often, Schweitzer's study is, though highly pertinent, unknown.

Further examination of how the Schweitzerian views gained such widespread reflection in liturgiology and sacramentology is therefore called for.

Even more pressing is reexamination of with what justification, in the history of research and exegetically, Schweitzer said what he did which has thus proven so unexpectedly influential. To read Schweitzer beckons one to explore further what he set forth in this part of his grandiose vision of the last/Lord's Supper, from Jesus to the patristic church, and to test his foundations on which others have, often unwittingly, built.

Bibliography

(Works mentioned in the Introduction or important for the subject)

A. Works by Albert Schweitzer:

(Original German edition cited, plus reprinting in Schweitzer's *Gesammelte Werke* [ed. R. Grabs, Munich], and English translations where these exist)

On the New Testament

1901   *Kritische Darstellung unterschiedlicher neuerer historischer Abendmahls-auffassungen.* Frieburg in Breisgau: C. A. Wagners Universitäs Buchdruckerei. Dissertation for the licentiate degree. Basically Part I of the next title.

1901   *Das Abendmahl im Zusammenhang mit dem Leben Jesu und der Geschichte des Urchristentums.* Two volumes. Tübingen: J. C. B. Mohr (Paul Siebeck). Second edition, photomechanically reproduced, 1929.

       Heft 1. Das Abendmahlsproblem auf Grund der wissenschaftlichen Forschung des 19. Jahrhunderts und der historischen Berichte. Translated below.

       Heft 2. Das Messianitäts- und Leidensgeheimnis: Eine Skizze des Lebens Jesu. Werke, 5, pp. 195-340. Translated by Walter Lowrie, *The Mystery of the Kingdom of God: The Secret of Jesus' Messiahship and Passion.* London: A. & C. Black; New York: Dodd, Mead & Co., 1914. Reprinted, 1925; New York: Macmillan, 1950; New York: Schocken Books, 1964. The 1950 edition is cited above.

1906   *Von Reimarus zu Wrede: Eine Geschichte der Leben-Jesu-Forschung.* Tübingen: J. C. B. Mohr (Paul Siebeck). Translated by W. Montgomery, *The Quest of the Historical Jesus: A Critical Study of its Progress from Reimarus to Wrede.* London: A. & C. Black, 1910. Often reprinted. We cite the 1968 paperback edition (New York: Macmillan), with a new introduction by James M. Robinson.

1911   *Geschichte der paulinischen Forschung von der Reformation bis auf die Gegenwart.* Tübingen: J. C. B. Mohr (Paul Siebeck). Translated by W. Montgomery, *Paul and His Interpreters: A Critical History.* London: A. & C. Black: New York: Macmillan, 1912, reprinted 1948 and 1956; Schocken Books, 1964.

1913   *Geschichte der Leben-Jesu-Forschung.* Tübingen: J. C. B. Mohr (Paul Siebeck). *Werke*, 3. Expanded edition of *Von Reimarus zu Wrede.* The new material has never been translated.

        Die psychiatrische Beurteilung Jesu: Darstellung und Kritik. Tübingen: J. C. B. Mohr (Paul Siebeck). Second edition, 1933. Translated by W. Montgomery, "The Sanity of the 'Eschatological Jesus'," *The Expositor*, Eighth series, 6 (1913):328-42, 439-55, 554-68. Translated by Charles R. Joy, *The Psychiatric Study of Jesus: Exposition and Criticism.* Boston: Beacon Press, 1948.

1930   *Die Mystik des Apostels Paulus.* Tübingen: J. C. B. Mohr (Paul Siebeck). *Werke,* 4, pp. 15-510. Translated by W. Montgomery, *The Mysticism of Paul the Apostle.* London: A. & C. Black; New York: Henry Holt, 1931; New York: Seabury, 1968.

1967   *Reich Gottes und Christentum,* edited by Ulrich Neuenschwander. Tübingen: J. C. B. Mohr (Paul Siebeck). *Werke,* 4, pp. 511-731. Translated by L. A. Garrard, *The Kingdon of God and Primitive Christianity.* London: A. & C. Black; New York: Seabury, 1968.

Autobiographical

1924   *Aus meiner Kindheit und Jugendzeit.* Munich: C. H. Beck. *Werke,* 1, pp. 253-313. Translated by C. T. Campion, *Memoirs of Childhood and Youth.* London: Macmillan, 1925.

1931   *Aus meinem Leben und Denken.* Leipzig: F. Meiner, 1931. *Werke,* 1, pp. 252. Translated by C. T. Campion, *Out of My Life and Thought.* London: Allen & Unwin; New York: Henry Holt, 1933.

B. Works about Schweitzer

Grässer, Erich. *Albert Schweitzer als Theologe.* Beiträge zur historischen Theologie, 60. Tübingen: J. C. B. Mohr (Paul Siebeck), 1979.

Griffith, Nancy Snell, and Laura Person, *Albert Schweitzer: An International Bibliography.* Boston: G. K. Hall, 1981.

Groos, Helmut. *Albert Schweitzer, Grösse und Grenzen: Eine kritische Würdigung des Forschers und Denkers.* Munich: Ernst Reinhardt, 1974.

Kümmel, W. G. "Die 'konsequente Eschatologie' Albert Schweitzers im Urteil der Zeitgenossen." In Kümmel's *Heilsgeschehen und Geschichte: Gesammelte Aufsätze 1933-1964,* edited by E. Grässer, O. Merk, and A. Fritz. Marburg: Elwert, 1965. Pages 328-39.

Picht, Werner. *Albert Schweitzer: Wesen und Bedeutung.* Hamburg: Meiner, 1960. Translated by Edward Fitzgerald, *The Life and Thought of Albert Schweitzer.* New York: Harper & Row, 1964.

Reumann, John. " 'The Problem of the Lord's Supper' as Matrix for Albert Schweitzer's 'Quest of the Historical Jesus'." *New Testament Studies* 27 (1980-1981):475-87.

Seaver, George. *Albert Schweitzer: The Man and His Mind.* New York: Harper, 1947.

C. Works on the Lord's Supper and the New Testament

Averbeck, Wilhelm. *Der Opfercharakter des Abendmahls in der neueren evangelischen Theologie.* Konfessionskundliche und kontroverstheologische Studien, 19. Paderborn: Bonifacius-Druckerei, 1967.

Brilioth, Yngve. *Eucharistic Faith and Practice: Evangelical & Catholic.* Translated from the Swedish by A. G. Hebert. London: S.P.C.K., 1930.

Cullmann, Oscar. *Early Christian Worship.* Translated by A. S. Todd and J. B. Torrance. Studies in Biblical Theology, 10. London: SCM, 1953.

Feld, Helmut. *Das Verständis des Abendmahls.* Erträge der Forschung, 50. Darmstadt: Wissenschaftliche Buchgesellschaft, 1976.

Goguel, Maurice. *L'eucharistie des origines à Justin Martyr.* Paris: Fischbacher, 1910.

Lowrie, Walter. *Action in the Liturgy. Essential and Unessential.* New York: Philosophical Library, 1953.

Macgregor, G. H. C. *Eucharistic Origins: A Survey of the New Testament Evidence.* London: James Clarke, 1928.

Patsch, Hermann. *Abendmahl und historischer Jesus.* Stuttgart: Calwer Verlag, 1972.

Pesch, Rudolf. *Das Abendmahl und Jesu Todesverständnis.* Quaestiones Disputatae 80. Freiburg: Herder, 1978. Following his extensive commentary treatment, *Das Markusevangelium* (1976-1977), and a popular presentation, *Wie Jesus das Abendmahl hielt: Der Grund der Eucharistie* (1977; all published by Herder Verlag), Pesch argues, like Schweitzer, for the priority and basic historicity of the Marcan account of events in the upper room, but takes 14:25 not as a messianic banquet promise (as Schweitzer did) but rather as an amen-saying prophesying death and resurrection with certitude. English summary of Pesch's views in Robert J. Daly, "The Eucharist and Redemption: The Last Supper and Jesus' Understanding of his Death." *Biblical Theology Bulletin* 11 (1981): 21-27; and J. Reumann, "The Last and the Lord's Supper," in the *Bulletin* of the Lutheran Theological Seminary, Gettysburg PA, 1982 (Luther Colloquium 1981 issue).

Réville, Jean. *Les origines de l'eucharistic, messe, saint cène.* Paris, 1908.

Schleiermacher, Friedrich Ernst Daniel. *Die christliche Glaube nach den Grundsätzen der evangelischen Kirche im Zusammenhang dargestellt.* Berlin: Reimar, 1821-1822. Often reprinted. Translation of the second German edition, edited by H. R. Mackintosh and J. S. Stewart: *The Christian Faith, Presented in its Inner Connections according to the Fundamentals of the Evangelical Church.* Edinburgh: T. & T. Clark, 1948; Harper Torchbooks edition, New York, 1963.

Schweizer, Eduard. "Abendmahl: I. Im N(euen) T(estament)." *Die Religion in Geschichte und Gegenwart,* third edition (Tübingen: J. C. B. Mohr (Paul Siebeck), volume 1 (1957): columns 10-21. Translated by James M. Davis, *The Lord's Supper According to the New Testament.* Facet Books, Biblical Series, 18. Edited, with introduction, by J. Reumann. Philadelphia: Fortress, 1967. The notes cite much of the recent literature to which it is not possible to refer here.

Wainwright, Geoffrey. *Eucharist and Eschatology.* London: Epworth, 1971.

Wrede, William. *Das Messiasgeheimnis in den Evangelien: Zugleich ein Beitrag zum Verständnis des Markusevangeliums.* Göttingen: Vandenhoeck & Ruprecht, 1901. Translated by J. C. G. Greig, *The Messianic Secret.* Library of Theological Translations. Cambridge & London: James Clarke, 1971.

The Problem of the Lord's Supper
Volume I

by Albert Schweitzer

Preface to a New Investigation of the Lord's Supper

The impetus to the present work emanated from Schleiermacher. In 1897 I was assigned as the theme for my written examination* the following exercise: "Schleiermacher's Doctrine of the Lord's Supper Shall Be Described and Compared with the Interpretations Found in the New Testament and in the Confessional Writings."

I had not previously been concerned with the problem of the Lord's Supper, and I was not at all familiar with the latest research. I also had no time to make up for this deficiency, because the work had to be handed in within eight weeks. Therefore I was directed solely to the texts and to the creedal formulations of the various confessions.

For me, however, Schleiermacher's dialectic took the place of everything else. He so analyzes the problem that it stands before the reader as a whole and at the same time in all its details. We need only to

---

*Schweitzer's first examination in theology, completed in 1898. —J. R.

[To facilitate comparison, the page numbers of the German original are inserted in the outside margins.]

take as serious history the dialectical game which he plays with consummate skill to calm and conciliate the people's minds and to delight his own aesthetic sense, and then we arrive precisely at the standpoint of modern historical investigation.

One sentence is decisive here. In Section 139.3 of his dogmatic theology,* Schleiermacher speaks of the external development of our celebration of the Lord's Supper and shows how we, in accordance with the nature of the celebration, must limit ourselves to essential features when we reproduce the historical particulars. If we wanted, for example, to put a special emphasis on the close relation the historical meal had with the passover meal, then we would immediately be forced to conclude "that the Lord's Supper can never again be as Christ instituted it, and therefore it really could not have been ordained by him as an independent and permanent institution for the Church." "This uncertainty," he then continues, "is so obvious that it can easily make itself better known in the Evangelical (Protestant) Church now than was previously the case, and it naturally raises the question of what our faith really rests on in this matter. It hardly can be maintained that this intention to institute a permanent rite emanates distinctly from the words of Christ which have been preserved for us. On the contrary, some of our narratives (Mark and Matthew) contain no such command at all, and in the others (Luke and Paul) it is only indistinctly expressed. And since the apostles inferred no such command from the words of Christ at the foot-washing, they would also have had the right to make no more of a definite and universal institution out of the Lord's Supper than they did out of the foot-washing! But since it is now obvious that they did the one and not the other, we can adhere to the practice which they established, without our having to decide whether Christ gave them yet other explicit instructions concerning the Lord's Supper, or whether they inferred the same from his words, or whether simply by their direct impressions of the occasion and by the accompanying circumstances they were led to make a permanent institution out of the Lord's Supper but not out of the foot-washing. In the latter case, we would not then be able to

vi

---

*ET: *The Christian Faith, Presented in Its Inner Connections according to the Fundamentals of the Evangelical Church,* edited by H. R. Mackintosh and J. S. Stewart (Edinburgh: T. & T. Clark, 1948); and, two volumes, with an introduction by Richard R. Niebuhr (New York: Harper Torchbooks, 1963). —J. R.

regard the Lord's Supper in quite the same sense as directly instituted by Christ, but we would still have to go on believing that they acted in accordance with his intention, if we do not also want to give up their canonical authority in a matter at the very heart of their calling."

In the final analysis, our celebration of the Lord's Supper does not rest on an explicit command of Jesus! Grafe* is therefore completely innocent! What he as an honest historian, following other historians and compelled by the weight of the facts, expressed cautiously and considerately, Schleiermacher threw boldly into his dogmatic theology. But whereas people sympathetically nodded to the refined game of the dialectician, they were quite displeased with the respected historian when he dared to say approximately the same thing. Perhaps Grafe's temperamental opponents overlooked this page in their Schleiermacher, or they held that the section in question, because it   vii was written quite some decades ago, may also pass as orthodox in ambiguous matters. It is remarkable: In theology today you may say almost anything you please, if you do it politely and cleverly, with a certain refined skepticism. But people are severe with the honest person who speaks because his conscience compels him to do so.

The proposition which Schleiermacher expressed quite clearly for the first time, but which was then ignored for decades, is suited to "awaken us out of our dogmatic slumber," in the Kantian sense.** That is to say, Schleiermacher's proposition shows that not only the ecclesiastical but even the scholarly interpretations of the Lord's Supper do not satisfy the actual facts of the case. The ecclesiastical interpretations presuppose that Jesus intended the celebration to be repeated, but they cannot prove that he really ordained it, since the command in question is missing from the oldest witnesses. On the other hand, a series of scholarly interpretations proceeds upon the basis that the celebration

---

*Eduard Grafe (1855-1922) was a Protestant theologian who became professor of New Testament at Bonn in 1890. His survey on "the most recent research on the original celebration of the Lord's Supper," published in 1895 and noted by Schweitzer, p. 13 (below, p. 76), was originally given as a lecture to some 112 area pastors during a Bonn "vacation course," 16-18 October 1894. His objective report on what scholars were saying stirred up vigorous opposition among conservatives against the "unbelieving professors." Cf. *Die Religion in Geschichte und Gegenwart*, first edition, volume 2 (1910), columns 858-59. —J. R.

**An allusion to a phrase from Immanuel Kant (1724-1804), on whose philosophy Schweitzer had written a previous doctoral dissertation. —J. R.

was not intended to be repeated, but then they cannot explain why it nevertheless came to be observed in the very first congregation—and that indeed is also an indubitable fact.

The connection between the two celebrations—the historical and the congregational—therefore remains equally incomprehensible, whether we connect them directly and causally with each other through the command of repetition, or whether we are satisfied with establishing a purely temporal succession and leave the matter of causality undecided. Schleiermacher is the Hume* of the question of causality in the problem of the Lord's Supper.

My comparison of the most varied and chronologically separated doctrines of the Lord's Supper with Schleiermacher's view led me to the question: What then is the constant factor in this continual change of interpretations? Is it not conceivable that all periods in which the problem of the Lord's Supper exerts influence are governed by the same laws, and that therefore the true historical interpretation must be tested by these laws?

Therefore after I had finished the work for my examination and had indicated in broad strokes the new interpretation whose outline I already had in mind, I set about to study thoroughly all periods involving the question of the Lord's Supper—the early Christian, the medieval, the Reformation, and the modern. I was determined not to publish my new interpretation until I had thoroughly studied all of the periods in the light of it, and was certain that it explains the entire history of the Lord's Supper from the historical celebration of Jesus down to the most recent times. This work has taken me four years. Thus it is not until the fall of 1901 that I am publishing, in connection with my survey and evaluation of the historical investigation of the Lord's Supper in the nineteenth century, what I was certain of, independently of modern research, already in the fall of 1897.

viii

I have developed the position of the problem of the scholarly study of the Lord's Supper in the nineteenth century because this period lies closest to us. But I could just as well have utilized any other period for this purpose, since the laws are the same in all periods.

---

*David Hume (1711-1776), Scottish philosopher, whose book on epistemology, *An Inquiry Concerning Human Understanding* (1748), included a section "On Miracles," raised sharply the question of biblical miracles as violations of the laws of nature. —J. R.

This work intends to do more than simply advance a new historical interpretation of the Lord's Supper. It pursues the practical purpose of setting forth the historical foundation of our modern celebration of the Lord's Supper and of historically justifying our present practice. It is of course not to be denied that our congregational celebration, according to the current state of scholarship, hangs in the air. If the command of repetition is not historically based, then what is our repetition supposed to mean?

To be sure, this concern troubles the believer but little at first, and that is as it should be. It is not the business of the people who walk over the bridge to be anxious about whether the foundations have been slowly undermined by the floods. Rather, that is the responsibility of the architects. Even if the architects notice a sinking of only one millimeter, they must immediately work against an eventual catastrophe, even if the matter at first seems to be completely inconsequential to the passersby. In the same way, theologians must observe the foundation of faith and heed whether or not the historical basis of the institution, which forms, as it were, the bridge from the perishable to the imperishable, is undermined by the stream of the time. Then the theologians must decide whether or not a foundation of our celebration of the Lord's Supper which is entirely different from the previous   ix
foundation becomes necessary because of the historical world view.

Schleiermacher has said that the uncertainty concerning our authority for the repetition of the Lord's Supper could easily make itself better known in the Evangelical (Protestant) Church than was previously the case. And if this happens now, what then? So long as the problem of the authorization and necessity of our celebration of the Lord's Supper is not scientifically resolved, then there can take place through the most trivial circumstances a dogmatic discussion of this question which will be extremely irritating and unpleasant to public opinion, in comparison to which the Grafe case would be only a short, idyllic prelude.

The worst aspect of it all would be that this discussion, when once dragged out into the public, would necessarily remain without result, for then the person who thinks in a scholarly way will have to raise this question again and again, whereas the person who is closer to the standpoint of ecclesiastical faith will necessarily refuse to consider the question. The latter correctly feels that such theoretical considerations must not threaten a celebration which is so sacred and solemn and which in its characteristic mode was historically established anew by primitive Christian usage. The defender will in fact even have history on his side. For if the Lord's Supper has been celebrated in the Christian church from the beginning on, then this fact, when examined wholly objectively, is unquestionably much more decisive than the lack of the command of repetition in two old accounts. We are confronted with a completely unexplainable antinomy, concerning which we must be very careful about drawing any inferences against our celebration, especially when we consider the fact that in so doing we are attacking a part of the oldest and most sacred essentials of the Christian faith. Let us rather assume at first that we do not have the key to the explanation of the historical celebration and the primitive Christian celebration or to the understanding of their connection.

It is the task of scholarship to attack dangerous questions before they disturb injudicious public opinion, to remove the fuel, and to do productive work quietly.

When Schleiermacher in his dogmatic theology summoned the parties (which at that time existed only in his dialectical fantasy) to appear before him, he demanded that they should "recognize the canonical authority of the apostles in a matter at the very heart of their calling." But in all seriousness we cannot agree to this compromise. An aphorism does not banish the ghost. We certainly and gladly want to show proper respect to the apostles, but we must not base our celebration of the Lord's Supper solely upon their canonical authority.

Let us put the question in the proper light. Our celebration of the Lord's Supper originates in the practice of the first congregation to which the apostles belong. Transposed into the realm of history, the question about "the canonical authority of the apostles in a matter at the very heart of their calling" therefore runs as follows: What were the motives which led the first congregation to observe a celebration of this kind which is associated with Jesus' last meal? Was that arbitrariness or necessity?

There follows a second question, which Schleiermacher failed to take into account. If the first congregation repeated the celebration for definite reasons, are these reasons still valid for us? Is there something in the historical celebration as such which makes it necessary that we too should somehow derive a celebration directly from it? Or is it merely a question of something traditional?

The answer of history to this question goes like this: It was an absolute necessity that the Lord's Supper came to be observed by the first congregation, in spite of the lack of a command of repetition, and this necessity is still valid for us. Our celebration is not based upon the historical tradition or on the unverifiable authority of certain persons, but directly on the historical celebration. Thus our Lord's Supper is authorized, imperative, and necessary in and of itself.

The new historical understanding, however, reconciles the various viewpoints, not only in respect to the question of the authorization of the Lord's Supper, but also in respect to the question of the meaning of our celebration.

No one can fail to see that our celebration is actually very inadequate and lifeless when it is only a matter of representing Jesus' two figurative sayings by reproducing a historical situation, where the pastor takes the place of Jesus and the faithful take the place of the disciples. On the other hand, the confessional interpretations make unreasonable demands on earnest Christians, for these interpretations train such believers to be either thoughtless or unscrupulous, and they actually evoke doubt and scorn.

If both interpretations could break loose from the confines of their language, they would agree that the meaning of the celebration is something mysterious, where the individual enters into a special holy relationship with the celebrating congregation and the personality of our Lord. Now, however, the unfortunate "words of institution" compel one person through the pure symbolical interpretation not to come up to this mystery, and they compel another through the literal interpretation to go beyond this mystery and to maintain the incomprehensible. In this situation the attempts at mediation are worst of all. They may be correct in subject matter and according to their religious content, but in the interpretation of the figurative sayings they are cramped and artificial, so that a person with an honest mind cannot endure them. As the "words of institution" stand, and according to the role which was previously attributed to them in the celebration, only the pure symbolical interpretation or the crass realistic interpretation was allowable. Any mediating interpretation is untenable.*

Also here the true historical understanding brings freedom from this unnatural alternative, for it shows that the position which is

---

*The German, *Was dazwischen ist, ist vom Übel*, suggests Matthew 5:37 in the Luther Bible, *Was drüber ist, das ist vom Übel.* —J. R.

assigned to the figurative sayings in the whole of the celebration is historically false. The primitive Christian celebration is not based on the "words of institution"—this is my body, this is my blood—though these words had been spoken during the historical celebration. Therefore our interpretation is independent of these puzzling figurative sayings.

These brief suggestions should show that this work is written in a practical, edifying, and conciliatory spirit. To be sure, someone who comes from the customary interpretations will at first be much offended by this investigation, since it seeks to bring about reconciliation, not through a new confusion or obfuscation, but solely through historical veracity and impartiality. We must believe in history, that is, we must be confident that the deepening of faith and unity in faith are necessarily bound up with the progress of historical knowledge, although sometimes it does not appear this way at first. It is in this faith that I have begun and finished this investigation.

xii   This work appears in three books. The first book* treats the problem as it arises out of the research of the nineteenth century and out of the acounts. The second book** seeks the foundation of the historical celebration in the life and in the thought of Jesus. It presents itself as the sketch of a new life of Jesus. The third book*** treats the Lord's Supper in the primitive Christian and early Christian periods, and shows how, with equal justification and necessity, the Roman mass and the Greek mystery have developed out of it. The first and second books appear together. The third will follow these at the earliest opportunity.

In conclusion, I feel compelled to express my heartfelt thanks to all my friends who have helped me in this work: Pastors A. Ernst and R.

---

*The present work. —J. R.

**2. *Das Messianitäts- und Leidensgeheimnis: Eine Skizze des Lebens Jesu* (Tübingen: J. C. B. Mohr, 1901, 1929², 1956³); ET: Walter Lowrie, trans., *The Mystery of the Kingdom of God: The Secret of Jesus' Messiahship and Passion* (London: 1914, 1925²). —J. R.

***The third part never appeared because, as Schweitzer put it in 1931, *Von Reimarus zu Wrede (The Quest)* intruded. *The Quest*, Schweitzer said, originally intended only as a supplement to Part 2, became so bulky as to prevent his completing Part 3. See A. Schweitzer, *Out of My Life and Thought* (New York: Henry Holt, 1933), p. 47. —J. R.

Will of Strassburg, A. Huck and Ed. Unsinger of Schiltigheim, and Vicar Alfred Erichson of Strassburg.

Strassburg, August 1901.

Part One

The Problem of the Lord's Supper
according to the Scholarly Research
of the Nineteenth Century

Chapter I
Introduction

1. Skepticism in the Research on the Lord's Supper

There are questions which emerge in the thinking of mankind, claim the complete intellectual interest of a period, and then fade away. This happens even though these questions have not been solved, and even though it is not clear how interest in these questions could have been lost before they were solved.

Centuries pass by. Then, because of a turn in history, the same question again is thrust into the foreground and the game repeats itself.

To these intermittent "volcanoes" belongs the question of the Lord's Supper. Up until the present time three periods of action are to be noted. The first is the longest. It lasts about ten centuries. The intensity is in inverse ratio to the length. We have no mountain belching forth fire, but a crater with a slow outflow of lava. A few tremors—the Frankish controversies over the Lord's Supper—signify the end of this period of action.

The way in which the question appears anew in the time of the Reformation is most surprising. We would suppose that in the common opposition of all Reformation interpretations to the Roman theory the differences among Protestants, especially on this question, would remain latent for the time being. Instead, it is this very question of the Lord's Supper which becomes the pole around which thinking is oriented. This second dogmatic period was in its actual course just as short as it was violent. It hardly spans three decades. Then for dogmatics the question of the Lord's Supper becomes one question among others. Schleiermacher's dogmatic theology, the scholarly foundation of the attempts to reconcile the differences, treats it almost like an appendix.

The third period is introduced by historical-critical research. We are standing in the center of this period, but in such a position that the noonday already lies behind us. That is to say, exhaustion is already evident. A series of the most recently published essays were less confident than earlier studies that the problem can be solved by historical criticism. So an outspoken skepticism is now taking root, whose language can be perceived in Eichhorn's essay.[1]

There is something absolutely justified about this skepticism, namely, that it is based on the fact that with all the research of the nineteenth century the solution of the problem is farther away than ever. It is precisely through the historical-critical method that the difficulties have appeared to a much greater extent than anyone earlier would ever have suspected.

There is no justification, however, for taking a haughty attitude toward historical-scientific criticism, or for proclaiming that historical criticism, because it has not yet reached its goal of solving this problem, is inferior to an eccentric, hypercritical non-criticism. Instead of assuming such an attitude as that, we should search for the reasons why historical criticism could not previously lead us to the solution of this problem.

2. The Starting Point

The problem of the Lord's Supper consists of a series of individual

---

[1]"Das Abendmahl im Neuen Testament," by Albert Eichhorn (Leipzig 1898), Hefte zur "Christlichen Welt," no. 36.

questions, which in the various interpretations are answered differently, and are related to each other in different ways. Criticism usually revolves around these individual questions. Scholars investigate whether the setting of the words of institution is tenable and whether the exegesis of the figurative sayings is correct. They ask how the essay under consideration views the question of chronology, in what manner it substantiates the relationship which is affirmed or denied between the Lord's Supper and the Passover, and similar questions.　　3

In the following investigation the total conception and the relationship of the individual questions to one another are more important. Does a view of the Lord's Supper grow out of a series of independent decisions about the unanswered individual questions? Or are not these individual questions so bound up with one another through an obscure inner mechanism that if one is answered then the others are answered at the same time? What are the laws according to which the individual questions in the problem of the Lord's Supper are mutually conditioned? That is the question which concerns us. Only in this way can it be explained why the historical-critical method could not reach its goal.

3. The Individual Questions

Does the significance of the figurative sayings lie in the fact that Jesus breaks the bread and passes around the wine in the cup? Or does it depend on the fact that the disciples eat this bread and drink this wine?

Did he mean the words concerning the bread and wine as figurative sayings, or did he want to indicate by these words that the disciples through partaking of the bread and wine somehow assimilate his body and his blood?

Did the meal take place in connection with the Passover meal, so that Passover conceptions must be presupposed for Jesus' words and their understanding?

Does the chronology of the Gospels permit Jesus yet to be seen on Passover evening in the circle of the disciples?

Did he command the disciples to repeat the celebration?

What did he command them to repeat?

Is it possible that the "founder" required them to repeat his own words, which have meaning only in his mouth and in that historical moment?

Assuming that the command of repetition is not historical, how do we explain the fact that the disciples nevertheless come to repeat the celebration?

How is it possible that Paul in primitive Christianity introduces into his description of the historical celebration the repetition as going back to the Lord?

How do we explain the absence of the historical account from the Fourth Gospel, since chapter 6 obviously presupposes the celebration?

4   In general, is it not the case that if we accept the command of repetition, then it becomes impossible for us to understand the psychology of the historical celebration; whereas if we presuppose the absence of this command, then the repetition by the first congregation becomes quite incomprehensible?

If the Lord's Supper was held in conjunction with a Passover meal, how then can we understand the daily celebration in the primitive Christian period, either with or without the command of repetition?

Were the Agape and the Lord's Meal separated, were they somehow connected, or were they identical?

How in general did the celebration of the Lord's Meal develop in primitive Christianity? How are the statements of the Didache to be reconciled with the Pauline descriptions and requirements in 1 Corinthians 11?

What is the relationship between the information and the conception of the historical celebration which the Didache and Paul presuppose and the picture of the historical celebration in the Synoptics?

How can we explain the complete disappearance of the idea of suffering and of the situation of the historical celebration from the Didache?

Of what significance was the eschatological factor in the primitive Christian celebration of the Lord's Supper?

What is the connection between Jesus' concluding eschatological saying about drinking new wine in the kingdom of the Father and the course of the historical celebration?

How can the variations among the synoptic accounts be explained?

The Pauline description is chronologically the oldest; the Lucan text according to Codex D is the shortest: the Marcan text is found in connection with the simplest and most credible historical representation in the Gospels; and the Justinian account* is possibly independent

---

*That is, in Justin Martyr's *Apology.* —J. R.

of our Gospels. Which of these four basically different texts should we prefer?

For primitive Christianity, what was the relationship between participation in the Lord's Meal and the conception of redemption?

We assume that during the primitive Christian celebration the Lord's words were freely reproduced. There could be, however, only one meaning of these words. How can we explain the fact that we have no information about controversies over the meaning of these words in the whole primitive Christian period, indeed, actually not until the beginning of the Middle Ages? The insight that the conceptions of primitive Christianity still exhibited a certain degree of fluidity is not sufficient to explain the above fact.

4. The Four Types of Interpretations of the Lord's Supper

In our description of the scholarly debate about the Lord's Supper we first of all distinguish two main trends. We classify the studies according to whether they take as the basis of their interpretation the moment of presentation or the moment of partaking. By the moment of presentation we mean the action and words of Jesus during the historical celebration. By the moment of partaking we have in mind the significance of the eating and drinking by the participants, a significance which should grow out of the essence of the celebration. Besides the descriptions which one-sidedly develop one of these two moments while neglecting the other, there are yet other descriptions which are two-sided. These take one of the moments as their basis, but in doing so grant a secondary importance to the other moment. We have, therefore, four chief types in all, among which the widest variety of mediating positions are possible.

1. Interpretations with a one-sided development of the moment of presentation.*

2. Two-sided interpretations which take the moment of presentation as their basis and grant a secondary importance to the moment of partaking.

3. Interpretations with a one-sided development of the moment of partaking.

---

*On the terms here—*Darstellungs-* and (type 3) *Genussmoment*—see the Introduction, pp. 22-23. —J. R.

4. Two-sided interpretations which take the moment of partaking as their basis and grant a secondary importance to the moment of presentation.

The following description presents these interpretations in the order of their publication.

Chapter II
The Prelude: Zwingli and Calvin

To Zwingli belongs the credit for being the first to treat the problem of the Lord's Supper in a scholarly way. According to Zwingli, the significance of the historical celebration rests on the symbolical action of Jesus. By breaking the bread and offering the wine, the Lord proclaims his death. He ordains the repetition of the celebration so that Christians may remember his death over the broken bread and poured wine.

The weakness of Zwingli's interpretation lies in the fact that he places his chief emphasis solely upon Jesus' action. Zwingli can explain the historical celebration, but not the repetition, in which the stress necessarily does not rest on the action of Jesus but on the action of the participants in partaking of the bread and wine. Zwingli fails to enable us to understand why the disciples partook of the symbolical elements. He is even less successful in helping us to see why later generations also still eat and drink in connection with the repetition instead of merely watching in order to be edified by Jesus' action at the Lord's Supper while this action is being narrated and reenacted. The fact that Zwingli's teaching could not be theologically satisfying was, in the final analysis, the result of the one-sidedness of his scholarly exegesis.

Thus even from the viewpoint of scholarship Zwingli's interpretation had to be replaced by those views which could assign a place to the partaking by the participants in addition to the action of Jesus at the Lord's Supper, an action which is reenacted whenever the celebration is repeated. Such a view was supplied by Calvin's doctrine of the Lord's Supper.

For Calvin, the symbolism is based equally on what Jesus does with the elements (breaking of the bread and pouring out of the wine) and on what the participants do with them (eating of the bread and drinking of the wine). The scholarly strength of Calvin's doctrine of the Lord's Supper is due to his emphasis upon the offering and appropriation as the two fundamental moments of the Lord's Supper. Calvin's explanation of the historical celebration is not as satisfactory as Zwingli's. As a compensation for that deficiency, however, it is possible for Calvin to show clearly that the repetition of the Supper is necessary, since it is not solely the command of Jesus but the value Calvin places on the partaking which maintains the connection between the historical and the repeated celebration.

It was not only theological but also scholarly interests, therefore, which led to the victory of Calvin's interpretation of the Lord's Supper over that of Zwingli. The controversy between these two views was based in part on a scholarly foundation and formed a brief prelude to the great historical debate over the Lord's Supper in the nineteenth century.

7   Since the two-sided interpretation was widely spread owing to Calvin's victory over Zwingli, historical research presupposed this two-sidedness. Scholars placed their main emphasis upon the moment of presentation because exegetical clarity favored such an emphasis. Thus the two-sided interpretations which take the moment of presentation as their basis at first exhibited a distinct scholarly character.

Chapter III

The Two-Sided Interpretations
Which Take the Moment of Presentation
as Their Basis
and Grant a Secondary Importance
to the Moment of Partaking

1. The First Half of the Nineteenth Century:
De Wette, Ebrard, and Rückert.

[Wilhelm Martin Leberech de Wette (1780-1849), professor of exegesis at Heidelberg (1807), Berlin (1810), Basel (1822), who wrote on both the Old and New Testaments (complete exegetical handbook on all 27 books) as well as on dogmatics and practical theology. —J. R.]

[Johannes Heinrich August Ebrard (1818-1888), professor of Reformed Theology at Zurich and twice at Erlangen, with a period in between as consistorial counselor at Speyer, mentioned in Schweitzer's *Quest*, p. 116, for his pettifogging orthodoxy. —J. R.]

In his commentaries,[1] De Wette advocates the two-sided interpretation. The breaking and the eating of the bread, plus the pouring-out and the drinking of the wine, together determine the significance of the

---

[1]Cf. De Wette's *Commentar zu Matthäus* (1836) and *Commentar zu Johannes* (1837).

elements in the celebration. De Wette's chief emphasis, however, is on the breaking, the moment of presentation. His stress upon the moment of partaking is more of a secondary kind.

August Ebrard[2] places the same value on the partaking as on the breaking and the pouring-out. Both moments belong together and mutually condition each other. Jesus offers the broken bread to eat and the poured-out wine to drink.[3]

Ebrard's forceful emphasis upon the moment of partaking is understandable in light of his connection with the Reformed-Calvinistic interpretation. For purely scholarly reasons a stronger development of the same moment is found in Immanuel Rückert.[4] His classic writing sums up the whole output of the scholarly discussion of the question of the Lord's Supper in the first half of the nineteenth

8   century. The action of Jesus and the partaking on the part of the participants are stressed in the same way. In each of these two moments there is a special symbolism. Jesus breaks the bread and gives it to eat; he pours out the wine and offers it to drink.[5]

2. The Second Half of the Nineteenth Century:
Th. Keim, K. v. Weizsäcker, W. Beyschlag, H. Holtzmann, P. Lobstein, W. Schmiedel.

In the second half of the nineteenth century criticism follows a broad and quiet stream which carries both moments with it, yet in such a way that the moment of presentation forms the undercurrent, the moment of partaking, the upper current. The following remarks indicate the direction of the stream.

Th. Keim, *Geschichte Jesu von Nazara*, 1872.
Volume 3, pp. 232-90 ("Das Nachtmahl Jesu").

[(Karl) Theodor Keim (1825-1878), professor at Zurich and Giessen, was a pupil of F. C. Baur who wrote a three-volume life of Jesus which achieved amazing popularity. Rationalistic, psychologizing, and artistic, the book was regarded by Schweitzer (*Quest*, pp. 211-14) as very important: "nothing deeper or more beautiful has since

---

[2]*Das Dogma vom heiligen Abendmahl und seine Geschichte,* by Dr. August Ebrard. Two volumes, 1845.

[3]Cf. volume 1, pp. 79-120.

[4]*Das Abendmahl, sein Wesen und seine Geschichte in der alten Kirche*, by Dr. Leopold Immanuel Rückert, professor in Jena, 1856.

[5]Cf. volume 1, pp. 61-131.

been written about the development of Jesus" (p. 214). ET, by A. Ransom and E. M. Geldart, *The History of Jesus of Nazara* (London: Williams and Norgate, 1873-1874). —J. R.]

"We have the impression that for Jesus it was a question of something more than merely displaying before his guests a striking symbol of his body, which was to be broken and killed and in some way was to bring salvation to the disciples. We get the impression of a gift. This gift in the first place means that Jesus in an emphatic, definitive way speaks of the salvation of the disciples as the purpose of his impending death. And in the second place this gift means that in connection with these words he entrusts the symbols of this salvation to the heirs of this salvation, not only to observe but actually to take and to partake of. He deposits the possession of his saving death and its fruits in their hands" (p. 272).

Karl v. Weizsäcker, *Apostolisches Zeitalter*, 1896, pp. 596-602.

[Karl (or Carl) (von) Weizsäcker (1822-1899) succeeded F. C. Baur as professor of Church History at Tübingen. *Das Apostolische Zeitalter* appeared first in 1886. ET, *The Apostolic Age of the Christian Church,* translated from the second German edition by James Millar (London: Williams and Norgate, 1895-1897); see volume 2, pp. 279-86 especially 282. Schweitzer discusses Weizsäcker in his *Quest,* especially pp. 200-202, and in *Paul and his Interpreters,* pp. 23, 64-66. —J. R.]

Weizsäcker advocates an interesting distinction between the symbols of the two acts. The bread is the symbol of the presence of Christ in the congregation; the wine, however, is the symbol of his death, through which he has become the new passover sacrifice (p. 598).

W. Beyschlag, *Das Leben Jesu*, 1893. Volume 2, pp. 434-42.

[Willibald Beyschlag (1823-1900) was professor at Halle. Schweitzer discusses his "liberal" life of Jesus in his *Quest*, pp. 193, 215-26. —J. R.]

"The meaning of the institution of the Lord's Supper is perfectly clear: his body, which is broken for us; his blood, which is shed for us, is his life, which he gives us in his death. He gives up his life for us, so 9 that it may become effective in us; so that it, appropriated by the inner man, as the outer man assimilates food and drink, may become for him food and drink of eternal life, and thus effect in us the redemption which has come in him, the new covenant which has come in him, the new covenant of fellowship with God" (p. 439).

H. Holtzmann, *Biblische Theologie*, 1897.
Volume 1, pp. 296-304.

[Heinrich Julius Holtzmann (1832-1910) was Schweitzer's teacher at Strassburg, particularly famed for his work on the Synoptics, arguing for the priority of Mark; *Quest*, pp. 193, 202-205. —J. R.]

"The historical presupposition and universal result of recent studies is that Jesus offered his disciples bread and wine to partake of and in so doing spoke, with reference to the broken bread, of his body, and, with reference to the poured-out wine, of his blood, and at the same time especially designated the latter as the blood of the covenant" (p. 296).

Paul Lobstein, *La doctrine de la sainte cène*, Lausanne, 1899.

[Though Paul Lobstein (1850-1922) wrote many of his works in French, he was a German Protestant from the Vosges who was professor at Strassburg from 1884 on. —J. R.]

"This is my body," says Jesus while breaking the bread which he distributes to his disciples; "this cup is the new covenant in my blood shed for you," he says to them while passing around the cup (p. 46). The disciples must eat the bread which Jesus breaks for them and which he distributes to them: "Just as I invite you to eat this bread, so you are called to assimilate to yourselves the fruit of my death, the saving effects of that gift of myself, of my body broken and given up for you" (p. 47).

Wilhelm Schmiedel, "Die neuesten Ansichten über den Ursprung des Abendmahls," *Protestantische Monatshefte*, 3. Jahrgang, Heft 4, 1899.

[Paul Wilhelm Schmiedel (1851-1935) was professor at Zurich, writing extensively on exegetical and historical questions. Schweitzer, in his *Quest*, p. 278, notes him briefly and in his *Geschichte der Leben-Jesu-Forschung* (1913; reprinted, Hamburg: Siebenstern Taschenbuch Verlag, 1972), vol. 2, pp. 552-53, discussed Schmiedel's view on nine "pillar passages" in the gospels for a life of Jesus set forth in an article on "Gospels" for the *Encyclopaedia Biblica*. —J. R.

"The significance of the Lord's Supper is to be seen primarily in the breaking of the bread and in the pouring of the wine out of the pitcher into the cup. The distribution of these foods to be partaken of follows as a matter of secondary importance. So far as the main point was concerned, this distribution and partaking would not have been necessary, but since the participants formerly sat at the meal [in contrast to our present practices] it was natural" (p. 147).

The basic features which the above studies have in common are therefore as follows: the bread and wine are the body and blood of Christ, because by them he symbolizes his death and its saving value. At the same time he invites the disciples to partake, which is supposed to mean that the benefits of his death are for their good, if they understand that they are to make these benefits their own. The repetition came about in part because the religious value of this observance was perceived by the participants; in part because Jesus called upon 10 them to do so by a command or an intimation. These scholars stress the connection between the Lord's Supper and the Passover. They nevertheless do not declare that this connection is absolutely necessary' to their interpretations. On the whole these studies are quite shaky. They combine the most varied viewpoints with one another, with the result that it is almost impossible to summarize them accurately in a few words.

Therefore it is also not advisable to start with these studies in order to establish the laws which govern the connection between the individual questions. The crisis in this situation was first brought to light by the interpretations which take the moment of partaking as their basis.

Chapter IV

Survey of the Interpretations Which Take the Moment of Partaking as Their Basis

If we choose from the history of the scholarly research on the Lord's Supper the works which in a general way take the moment of partaking as their basis, then the following names are joined together in a motley, disconnected series: David Fr. Strauss, Bruno Bauer, E. Renan, Adolf Harnack, Fr. Spitta, W. Brandt, Erich Haupt, Friedrich Schultzen, Rich. Ad. Hoffman, and Albert Eichhorn. In this series we have no natural continuity, as in the series previously observed. Upon closer examination, two periods appear. The first occurs in the middle of the century (Fr. Strauss, Bruno Bauer, E. Renan). The second commences at the beginning of the nineties (Harnack and Spitta) and comes before the close of the decade to its natural conclusion (A. Eichhorn).

Strauss, Bruno Bauer, E. Renan, W. Brandt, Spitta, and Eichhorn offer interpretations with a one-sided development of the moment of partaking. Adolf Harnack, Erich Haupt, Friedrich Schultzen, and R.

A. Hoffmann advocate the two-sided interpretations which take the moment of partaking as their basis and grant a secondary importance to the moment of presentation.

Chapter V

The Interpretations
with a One-Sided Development
of the Moment of Partaking

1. The Early Period: Fr. Strauss, Bruno Bauer, E. Renan.

[David Friedrich Strauss (1808-1874) studied under F. C. Baur and taught briefly at Tübingen until controversy over his book on Jesus forced him from an academic career. Schweitzer devotes two chapters to him in his *Quest*, pp. 78-120, besides pp. 193-200 in his later (1864) "Life of Jesus for the German People." ET of the work cited above, *The Life of Jesus Critically Examined*, translated from the fourth German edition by George Eliot (Mary Ann Evans) (London: Chapman Brothers, 1846; reprinted, Philadelphia: Fortress, 1972), pp. 631-34. —J. R.]

[On Bruno Bauer (1809-1882), a conservative who became a radical critic, see Schweitzer's *Quest*, pp. 137-60. —J. R.]

[Though Ernst Renan (1823-1892), the French Catholic seminarian who became a renowned orientalist and liberal biblical scholar, fares badly in Schweitzer's judgment (*Quest*, pp. 180-92), his *Vie de Jésus* enjoyed wide popularity; it is translated as *The Life of Jesus* by C. E. Wilbour (London: Trübner, 1864) and by W. G. Hutchinson (London: W. Scott, 1897; often reprinted). —J. R.]

For the interpretations with a one-sided development of the moment of partaking there are two periods. The first occurs around the middle of the nineteenth century; the second, toward the end of that century. Friedrich Strauss is characteristic of the first; Friedrich Spitta, of the second.

Strauss[1] argues that the translation "this signifies," if it is supposed to refer to that which Jesus does with the elements, does not at all suffice, indeed can by no means have been in the minds of the authors of the Gospels. "To the writers of our Gospels the bread of the Lord's Supper was the body of Christ . . . if anyone had concluded that the bread merely signifies the body, the Gospel writers would not have been satisfied with that conclusion" (pp. 436ff.). It is inadmissible from the standpoint of critical scholarship to think that Jesus foresaw with certainty his violent death. For Jesus, therefore, the symbolism of his last meal with his disciples cannot at all refer to his death. Likewise we must regard the commandment of repetition as unhistorical. The inauthenticity of this command is supported by the silence of the first two Gospels and the consideration that in general a memorial celebration more naturally grows out of the needs of those who remain behind than from the plan of the departed one. This last meal with the disciples was also not a Passover meal. The only historical feature in the entire tradition is the concluding eschatological saying over the cup: "I shall no more drink of it until I drink it new with you in my Father's kingdom." In Jesus' thought this saying refers to the next Passover wine, not to eating and drinking in general. In accordance with the conceptions of his time, Jesus often spoke of meals in the messianic kingdom, and thus he may have expected that in the kingdom the Passover meal in particular would be celebrated with peculiar solemnity. When he now assures his disciples that he will no more partake of this meal in this age but only in the new age, then the messianic kingdom must, according to his expectation, begin before the celebration of the Passover. But this expectation does not require us to suppose that Jesus thought that the appearance of the kingdom was connected with his death. The entire primitive Christian conception of the Lord's Supper is explained by the fact that—instead of the messianic kingdom and its Passover celebration—the death of Jesus occurred.

The church celebrated the Passover. It was natural that the attempt

---

[1]David Fr. Strauss, *Das Leben Jesu*. 1st edition, Tübingen, 1836. Volume 1, pp. 396-442, "Das Abendmahl."

had to be made to give a Christian meaning to the Passover by relating it to the death and last meal of Jesus (which was no Passover meal). In this way Strauss explains the intrusion of the idea of the passion and the prophecy of suffering into the historical accounts of the Lord's Supper. The elements were related to the body and blood of Christ. At the same time, Jesus' saying about partaking of the Passover wine was related to eating and drinking in general and connected with bread and wine as his body and blood. Thus originated the idea of the command of repetition. The tendency to detach the meal of commemoration from the Passover and to observe it frequently explains how such a saying came into use.

This ingenious interpretation of Fr. Strauss already contains all the factors which characterize the later interpretations of the Lord's Supper which one-sidedly stress the moment of partaking. Above all, Strauss takes into consideration the detachment of the historical celebration from the Passover meal; the elimination of the references to the passion from the sayings of Jesus; the explanation of the repetition of the celebration without the supposition of the command of repetition; and the necessity of explaining all of the features of the New Testament accounts of the Lord's Supper which are recognized as unhistorical (connection with the Passover festival, reference to the death of Christ, and the command of repetition) on the basis of the development of the primitive Christian celebration in a period of less than two decades.

If one does not want to prove Strauss' reconstruction by a bold historical construction, there remains nothing but some form of scholarly skepticism. This is the way taken by Bruno Bauer.[2] He presupposes that the accounts want to say: the Lord offered his disciples his body and his blood to partake of. The command of repetition is an addition from a later time with an attenuating tendency. It was felt that for the historical celebration the partaking could not be thus maintained. Therefore the reference to the future was stressed, which lies at the basis of the formula in itself. Jesus could not have offered his flesh and blood to his disciples to eat.[3] Therefore Mark's account is a

13

---

[2] Bruno Bauer, *Kritik der evangelischen Geschichte*, 1842. *Kritik der Evangelien*, 1850. Volume 3, pp. 191-213.

[3] *Kritik der evangelischen Geschichte*, Volume 3, p. 241: "A man who is sitting there physically and personally cannot arrive at the thought of offering others his body and his blood to partake of."

fantasy, and all other accounts are imitations of this invention.

How very straightforwardly Bauer executes his presupposition that the moment of partaking is basic, is shown by the way in which he reproaches Matthew for arbitrarily transforming the fact (confirmed by Mark) of the drinking on the part of the disciples into a command of Jesus, which transformation indicates a qualification. Bauer leaves the concluding eschatological saying unnoticed, and thus closes for himself the way which led Strauss out of the difficulties which the one-sided emphasis upon the moment of partaking carries along with it.

According to E. Renan,[4] Jesus on the last evening celebrated the usual common meal with the breaking of bread in the circle of his disciples. "In that repast, just as in many others, Jesus practices his mysterious rite of breaking bread." The concluding eschatological saying is doubtful and meaningless, for Renan. The synoptic accounts of the Lord's Supper are explained only by the development of later views, according to which the last meal was a Passover meal. In this way the idea of the passion, the reference of the elements to the body of Jesus, and the command of repetition forced their way into the description of the last meal.

2. The Modern Attempts: W. Brandt, Fr. Spitta, A. Eichhorn.

Compare with the following account the fateful report by E. Grafe ("Die neuesten Forschungen über die ursprüngliche Abendmahls-feier," *Zeitschrift für Theologie und Kirche*, 1895), and the clear summary by Rud. Schäfer *(Das Herrenmahl nach Ursprung und Bedeutung*, 1897).

[On Grafe, see the note above, on Schweitzer's Preface. Licentiate Rudolf Schäf-er's *Das Herrenmahl nach Ursprung und Bedeutung mit Rücksicht auf die neuesten Forschungen untersucht* (Gütersloh: C. Bertelsmann, 1897), was reviewed by Lobstein in *Theologische Literaturzeitung* 23 (1898): 291-93. —J. R.]

The last decade of the nineteenth century offers for the first time a study in which the ideas suggested by Strauss, Bauer, and Renan are developed with full clarity and logic into a unified picture. This is the epoch-making work of Spitta. The studies of Ad. Harnack and W. Brandt precede it chronologically in emphasizing the exclusive charac-ter of the historical celebration as a meal. Nevertheless, since Harnack is already more of a transition to the two-sided interpretations which

[4]E. Renan, *La vie de Jesus*, 1863, pp. 385ff.

take the moment of partaking as their basis, it is advisable not to treat him until then. In addition, in the third edition of his history of doctrine (volume 1, p. 64) he has expressed his view of Spitta's attempted solution and newly formulated his own position in the light of it.

3. W. Brandt

Die evangelische Geschichte und der Ursprung des Christentums. Leipzig, 1893, pp. 283ff.

[Wilhelm Brandt (1855-1915) was a Dutch Reformed pastor who after study in Strassburg and Berlin (1891-1892) became a member of the theology faculty in Amsterdam; *Quest*, pp. 242, 257-62. His radical views found favor with the "Christ myth" School. —J. R.]

The chief significance of the historical celebration lies in the communal partaking. By means of the figurative saying at the Lord's Supper Jesus made the common meals a symbol of the fellowship. In the meaning of this symbol is to be seen the basis of the repetition. An allusion to the death of Jesus, even if it is found in the saying which accompanied the breaking of bread, is meaningless so far as the essence of the celebration is concerned.

The incorporation of the idea of the passion and the introduction of the command of repetition into our accounts go back to a displacement in the primitive Christian celebration. This is conditioned by the fact that after the year 70, because of the lack of the lamb, the bread and cup formed the chief ingredients of the Jewish Passover meal, thus preparing the way for a conforming of the Passover to the primitive Christian celebration of the Lord's Meal. This situation explains the fact that the Jewish Passover influenced the Lord's Meal in its external course and thought content.

In Brandt's plausible sketch we find again the peculiarities—already noted by Strauss—of those interpretations which emphasize exclusively the moment of partaking. The command of repetition is missing, and it is a matter of tracing the reference to suffering in our accounts back to the incorporation of later ecclesiastical concepts. It is, however, questionable whether the way pointed out by Brandt really leads to the goal. It is certain that he did not consider a great difficulty: How could the disciples have understood the words of the Master in the sense offered above? How could they have understood at all that he, in offering them bread and wine, was inviting them to partake of his body and his blood? 15

Spitta has done invaluable service by bringing this question to the foreground of consideration.

4. Fr. Spitta

Die urchristlichen Traditionen über Ursprung und Sinn des Abendmahls (zur Geschichte und Litteratur des Urchristentums), 1893, pp. 207-337.

[Friedrich Spitta (1852-1924) was professor of New Testament and Pastoral Theology at Strassburg from 1887 till he moved from there to a chair at Göttingen, Germany, in 1919. His relationships with Schweitzer during the years when Schweitzer was student and lecturer there are noted above in the Introduction. Though known chiefly for his work as a liturgical scholar, Spitta is given rare accolades by Schweitzer not only for his views on the Lord's Supper but also for his discernment of Jewish backgrounds to Christianity elsewhere; e.g., *Paul and his Interpreters*, p. 52, n. 1 ("Among the few scholars who stem the tide of conventional stupidity Frederick [sic] Spitta deserves a foremost place," though the appeal is to his lectures, rather than published views) and pp. 148-49; *Geschichte der Leben-Jesu-Forschung*, pp. 593-95 and 609-10. —J. R.]

The meaning of Jesus' sayings lies purely and simply in the invitation to partake. According to his sayings, that which is partaken of is his body and his blood, precisely because it is partaken of! The breaking and pouring out as the representative action which is supposed to give to the elements an illustrative reference to his death, was far from his mind. The historical celebration was a meal at which, according to the common contents of all accounts, the disciples at his invitation were supposed to eat the food presented to them as his body and drink the wine poured out for them as his blood, and this they also did.

Strauss and Bruno Bauer had established the same facts of the case as offered by the sources, but from this position they were forced to call into question the historical reality of the procedure as portrayed in the Gospels and to explain the origin of the accounts, whether it be out of the history of primitive Christianity (Strauss), or whether it be out of the history of the origin of the Christian tradition generally (Bruno Bauer). The idea that the disciples at the invitation of Jesus should have partaken of his body and his blood at that time is, for Strauss and Bauer, impossible.

Spitta can uphold the procedure as historical with the aid of eschatological lines of thought. Establishing a link with the conception of the messianic covenant, Jesus—as the harmonious features of all accounts show—thought in connection with "the words of institution" of the eating and drinking at the messianic meal. In the prophetic, apocalyptic, sapiential, and rabbinic literature, the consummation of the kingdom is described in terms of the messianic meal, at which the food partaken of is the Messiah himself! On the basis of this concep- 16 tion Jesus could presuppose that the disciples would understand him when he invited them to partake of himself while eating. What he offers to them is an anticipation of the great messianic meal of the end-time. According to this conception they could eat the body of the Messiah and drink him in his blood, the juice of the grapes.

The last meal was no Passover meal; the thought of the passion did not come into question with respect to the symbolism of the elements; and the command of repetition is not historical. These views are of a later kind and are only understandable in light of the fact that as a consequence of the death of Jesus, which occurred in the meantime, the interpretation of his words at the last meal necessarily had to change. The celebration was regarded as analogous to the Passover meal, because it was now unavoidable that the sayings about his body and blood should be explained in terms of his sufferings. Along with this reinterpretation of these sayings, the conception of an institution necessarily forced its way in.

Paul kept the original interpretation in balance with the interpretation which referred to the passion. First Corinthians 10:1ff. and 10:14ff. do not yet know the thought of the passion, and stress the moment of partaking. In 1 Corinthians 11:23ff. the new factor appears, which Paul, in the course of his struggle against the agape scandal in Corinth, introduces into the celebration: the celebration has to do with Jesus' death.

The new feature introduced by Spitta is, therefore, his bringing into play peculiar eschatological lines of thought, by means of which he can uphold a celebration as historical in which the Master offers bread and wine to those reclining at table, with the invitation to eat his body and to drink his blood. The fact that the celebration was favorably received in the first congregation without an explicit command of repetition was grounded in the nature of the celebration. From this perspective it does not then seem impossible to understand how the factors appeared in the development which now follows—the factors which gave rise to the new features in the interpretation and evaluation of the celebration.

5. Criticism of Spitta's Interpretation

The great significance of Spitta's interpretation is due to the fact that he interpreted the problem of the Lord's Supper and undertook to solve it from one central perspective. For Spitta, all of the individual questions stand in a close reciprocal relationship. His discussion forms a closed chain, in which each part is taken into consideration only in connection with the others. In this feature lies the great advance of his investigation beyond earlier studies. The text-critical and the exegetical discussions are, for Spitta, both groundwork for and result of the total interpretation.

Spitta's interpretation has been called an eschatological one because he, like Fr. Strauss, employs the idea of the meal in the messianic kingdom in order to make the historical celebration understandable. In doing so Strauss started with the Synoptics' concluding eschatological saying, in which Jesus refers the disciples to the great meal of the end-time, where he will again be united with them. The eschatological character of Spitta's interpretation, however, is not based upon the synoptic saying but upon an eschatological conception of the end-time meal, which is brought together from the apocryphal and sapiential literature. Spitta's approach gives rise to a series of weighty contradictions with the Synoptics' concluding eschatological saying.

According to Spitta, the Messiah at the end-time meal offers himself to his own as food and drink. According to the Synoptics, Jesus points to the end-time meal where he partakes with them of the fruit of the vine. For Spitta, therefore, Jesus wants to be food and drink; for the Synoptics, Jesus is a table companion who shares in the partaking!

For Spitta, the eschatological reference is presupposed for the food as well as for the drink. At the historical celebration, however, the concluding eschatological saying refers only to the cup!

Spitta's eschatology refers to the invitation to partake of the body and blood. The Synoptic eschatological saying has no connection with the partaking, but follows only after the partaking.

Spitta's interpretation is, therefore, completely independent of the Synoptics' concluding eschatological saying. This saying also does not figure in Spitta's shortest form of the words of institution, but these simply read: "Take, eat, this is my body." "Drink you all out of it. This is the blood of my covenant, which is poured out for many."

These sayings constitute the celebration, for "in the congregation they always remembered how he at that time indicated that he is now 18 and in all eternity the proper food and refreshment for their souls" (Spitta, p. 289). Thus, for Spitta, the Synoptics' concluding eschatological saying becomes the sorrowful farewell saying, that forms the transition from the joyful sound of the eschatological mood which is confident of victory to the march toward death.

Christ the proper food of the soul: this thought is modern. Spitta's eschatology aims to let this idea play in an artificial, antique light, by means of a compilation of Old Testament and apocryphal sayings, in order that he may explain the invitation of Jesus to partake of his body and blood in the context of the historical situation. If we reject this artificial light, then only the darkness of skepticism remains. That is the case with Eichhorn.

6. A. Eichhorn

Das Abendmahl im Neuen Testament, "Hefte zur christlichen Welt," no. 36, 1898.

[Though Albert Eichhorn (1856-1926), associate professor at Halle and Kiel, published comparably little because of illness, his views, especially on the Lord's Supper from a history of religions point of view, were a stimulus to others. On the quotation above, cf. W. G. Kümmel, *The New Testament: The History of the Investigation of Its Problems,* translated by S. McLean Gilmour and Howard C. Kee (Nashville and New York: Abingdon, 1972), pp. 253-55. —J. R.]

"If we trust our records," Eichhorn suggests, Jesus celebrated the first Lord's Supper with his disciples in this way: he distributed to them bread and wine, and they ate and drank his body and his blood. The entire emphasis is upon the partaking. A symbolism which is based on Jesus' action cannot persist together with this stress on the partaking. We cannot say that the breaking of the bread indicates the breaking of the body and that the drinking of the wine points to the pouring out of the blood. The action which in reality is engaged in is simply the eating and drinking.

If these, then, are the facts of the case as presented in the sources, then there is for the present no possibility of understanding the historical celebration and how it came to be repeated. Whatever Jesus may have said and done on that evening, the cult-meal of the Church with the sacramental eating and drinking of the body and blood of Christ, as it developed in early Christendom almost from the beginning on, is not to be understood on that basis. Thus Eichhorn is necessarily forced into skepticism because he, in connection with the admitted significance of the moment of partaking, does not take into account eschatological or modern points of view.

Eichhorn's skepticism is due to his explicit refusal to understand the connection between the historical and the repeated celebrations on the basis of the available accounts, if a new fact, which is independent of our accounts, does not supply a datum which makes known the starting point of a development which we do not understand.—If we cannot succeed in identifying in the gnostic world of thought a sacramental meal, which could furnish the model for the Lord's Supper, so that for the earliest Christendom not the supranatural eating and drinking as such is new, but only the substitution of another supernatural substance through Christ's body and blood, then we must give up once and for all an understanding of the historical celebration and its development into the congregational celebration.

19

7. The New "Fact"

In order to escape this skepticism, Eichhorn postulates a new fact which goes beyond the contents of our sources. His predecessors, who in common with him stress exclusively the partaking, replace this postulate with an assumed fact.

D. Fr. Strauss explains the rise of the celebration of the Lord's Supper in primitive Christianity and thus the origin of our accounts by a misunderstanding on the part of the disciples of an eschatological saying spoken by Jesus at the final meal.

Bruno Bauer shifts the entire development, since he cannot explain it otherwise, to the fantasy of the proto-evangelist. Renan has recourse to the supposition that there was a mysterious rite of breaking bread which was already practiced earlier by Jesus and known to the disciples. Spitta brings to the Synoptic accounts a peculiar eschatological conception which is basically modern and which is not at all related to the concluding eschatological saying given by the Synoptics.

W. Brandt transfers modern conceptions into the thought-world of Jesus and his disciples, but he can find no basis in the accounts for this transferral.

Thus Eichhorn's investigation forms the natural conclusion to this series of interpretations which apparently is so disconnected, but which one-sidedly develops the moment of partaking. Through his dialectical handling of the problem, he removes in advance the justification for each future interpretation if it cannot introduce a new 20 historical fact which explains how the view arose that Jesus commanded the disciples to eat and to drink his body and his blood.

8. Skepticism as the Result of the One-Sided Development of the Moment of Partaking

Eichhorn's postulate also does not carry us any farther than do the facts asserted by his predecessors. He insists that the conception of the supranatural eating and drinking in an already existing religious thought-world be proved. In his view a better knowledge of "Gnosticism" could lead to such a proof.

If we grant that such a supranatural eating and drinking already existed, we still must show how it occurred to anyone in primitive Christianity to incorporate this thought into the Lord's Supper. To what extent did the historical celebration present a point of contact for such an incorporation? The operation proposed by Eichhorn hangs entirely in the air, for our accounts are altogether foreign and unreceptive to such a procedure.

Now the transformation of Eichhorn's postulate into a corresponding historical fact would be the only escape from skepticism. But even the first step shows that such an escape is completely hopeless. Therefore any interpretation which proceeds from the presupposition that Jesus (over bread and wine) invited his own to partake of his body and blood must from the outset and under all circumstances give up all claims to a solution of the problem.The thoroughgoing development of the moment of partaking necessarily leads to skepticism: that is the result of these interpretations.

9. The Logical Ground of Skepticism

If skepticism sets in during the course of the scholarly treatment of a question, that always follows from the fact that an unfounded proposition lies hidden among the presuppositions, a proposition which from then on teases human thinking and leads it astray. Scholarship in and of itself can never lead to skepticism. When the unproved proposition is discovered among the presuppositions, then the skepticism is removed.

Where then is this unproved proposition in the above studies? The error cannot be due to their exclusive emphasis upon the moment of

21 partaking. The facts that the Lord's Supper was taken over and celebrated by the primitive Christian Church as a meal, and that the action which connects the primitive Christian celebration with the historical one is not the symbolical action of the "Founder" but the action of the participants—the eating and drinking, are facts that are offered by the sources and confirmed by primitive Christianity.

The error is not to be sought in the fact of the evaluation of the moment of partaking, but in the manner of it. All of the above studies formulate the matter thus: that Jesus in offering the bread and wine invited the disciples to eat his body and drink his blood. The skepticism, therefore, is due to connecting the character of the celebration as a meal with the figurative sayings, for in doing so a statement is made in which subject and object are identical: the one who offers is simultaneously the one who is partaken of. Here thinking stops. The luxuriant creeper of historical and exegetical fancies is no bridge over the chasm of self-contradiction.

Instead therefore of starting with the statement that Jesus offered his disciples his body and his blood to partake of, we must begin by testing the presupposition itself. Is it really a fact (irrefutably established on the basis of the primitive Christian celebration and of the accounts) that Jesus required his own to partake of his body and blood in any form? If the answer is "Yes," then the solution to the problem of the Lord's Supper is impossible, since by that approach we can never explain the "how" on the basis of our texts, and every free interpretation remains without support from our accounts.

Chapter VI

21

The Two-Sided Interpretations Which Take the Moment of Partaking as Their Basis and Grant a Secondary Importance to the Moment of Presentation: Ad. Harnack, Erich Haupt, Fr. Schultzen, R. A. Hoffmann.

1. General

This series of two-sided interpretations is influenced by the interpretations which one-sidedly develop the moment of partaking. Whereas the direction which is indicated by the names Rückert, Lobstein, and Holtzmann sought to explain the partaking of the participants by starting with the action of Jesus, the new two-sided interpretations proceed conversely. They place the partaking in the foreground and then seek so to formulate and to stress this moment of partaking that Jesus' action which points to his death is also in some way or other consistent with, and receives its explanation from, the partaking. The emphasis is therefore shifted from the one side to the other.

In the final analysis it is exegetical considerations which lead this group of authors to take into account also the idea of the passion and the action of Jesus. "The words are too powerful for me," says Harnack in his evaluation of Spitta's interpretation. Harnack agrees with

22

Spitta's basic idea, but he is not satisfied with Spitta's exegesis. This is also the motto of the other two-sided interpretations.

2. Ad. Harnack

Brot und Wasser: die eucharistischen Elementen bei Justin ("Texte und Untersuchungen," volume 7, pp. 117ff., 1891); *Theologische Literaturzeitung*, 1892, pp. 373-78; *Dogmengeschichte* (3rd. edition), volume 1, p. 64. (*History of Dogma*, volume 1, p. 66.)

[Adolf (von) Harnack (1851-1930), the famed church historian, was professor at Berlin. Schweitzer mentions his generally liberal noneschatological views in his *Quest*, pp. 243, 252-53, 316; *Geschichte*, passim, e.g., pp. 543, 597-98; and *Paul and his Interpreters*, many times. The *Dogmengeschichte* reference above can be found in Harnack's *History of Dogma*, translated from the third German edition by Neil Buchanan (Boston: Roberts Brothers, Little, Brown, 1895-1900; reprinted New York: Dover Publications, 1961), Vol. 1, p. 66, n.1. —J. R.]

Through an investigation as to whether water or wine was the eucharistic element to be partaken of in the early church, Harnack in 1891 came to stress in a decisive manner his contention that in that earlier time the symbolism could not have referred to the essence of the elements but that the entire significance of the historical and of the primitive Christian celebrations was based upon the meal as such.

The Lord's Supper must have been an actual meal. The action in question is the eating and drinking. Jesus' sayings refer to the partaking. "The Lord sanctified the most important function of natural life when he designated the food as his body and blood. In this way for the sake of his own he placed himself forever in the midst of their natural life and directed them to make the preservation and the growth of this natural life into the power which promotes the growth of the spiritual life."

Harnack now seeks to bring into relationship with this factor yet another factor and in this way to make specific this general religious evaluation of the partaking. "The Lord instituted a memorial meal of his death, or rather, he designated (through the forgiveness of sins) the bodily food as his flesh and his blood, that is, as the food of the soul, if this food is partaken of with thanksgiving in memory of his death."

This sentence is decisive for Harnack's interpretation. "Or rather," "that is," and "if" are the sidings to which we transfer when coming from the general, wonderfully deep thought "that the Lord sanctified the most important function of natural life," in order to gain entrance to the historical celebration with the thought of the passion expressed there. The general meal character of his interpretation is therefore more precisely defined by the following propositions:

1. It is a matter of an institution.
2. The command of repetition is somehow contained in the historical situation.
3. The celebration refers to the death of the Founder.

3. Erich Haupt

Über die ursprüngliche Form und Bedeutung der Abendmahlsworte. Halle, Universitätsprogramm, 1894.

[A professor of New Testament exegesis at Halle, Erich Haupt (1841-1910) is described elsewhere by Schweitzer (*Quest*, pp. 251-52) as treating Jesus' eschatological sayings in such a way that modern mysticism is woven into them. —J. R.]

When Jesus offers the bread and wine to his disciples, who are reclining at table, and invites them to partake of his body and his blood, he intends to say, "My person is the bearer of the powers of a higher life. This life wants to be assimilated and become a component part of your persons, as is the case with your earthly food. This, however, is especially true of my imminent death. Precisely the sacrifice of my personality will disclose to you to the fullest extent the powers of life and salvation which are locked up within you and give the benefit of them to you." Haupt's basic thought is altogether identical with Spitta's. But whereas Spitta gave it an eschatological twist in the mouth of Jesus, Haupt employs the idea of the passion to apply this train of thought (which is characterized as modern by the expression "personality") to the historical celebration.

In this process, eschatology completely fades away. At the last meal Jesus has also spoken of the great meal of the consummation. Because the entire meal was now imitated, these eschatological thoughts also found their place. Thus Haupt does not use the eschatological factor to explain the repetition, but only on the basis of the repetition does the eschatological factor itself become understandable.

Through his secondary stress upon the idea of the passion to explain the celebration, Haupt is able to retain the command of repetition. On the night in which he was betrayed, the Lord viewed the entire meal as a farewell meal. He wants his memorial to be kept as a vigil during the period of separation. "Therefore there is not only no objection to the view that Jesus commanded his disciples to repeat the

24

observance, but a saying referring to repetition is even on inner grounds highly probable." Haupt's cautious and reserved grounding of his retention of the command of repetition provides the exact graduator for the influence of the moment of partaking (which Haupt takes as the basis of his interpretation) through the moment of presentation and the idea of the passion.

With the same caution, Haupt expresses himself about the relation between the repeated Lord's Meal and the Agape. "These common meals should not have two parts, a profane for feeding the body, and a religious, dedicated to the remembrance of Christ's death, but the entire meeting is supposed to bear a religious character, and the Lord's Meal in the narrower sense is only the high point of the whole."

4. Fr. Schultzen

Das Abendmahl im Neuen Testament. Göttingen, 1895.

[*Das Abendmahl im Neuen Testament*, by Licentiate Fr. Schultzen (Göttingen: Vandenhoeck & Ruprecht, 1895), was reviewed by Lobstein in *Theologische Literaturzeitung* 21 (1896): 234-37. —J. R.]

In Schultzen's interpretation, the emphasis upon the idea of the passion, and with it the significance of the moment of presentation in the action of Jesus, is moved up from a secondary position to a position of almost equal rank with the moment of partaking, but in such a way that the moment of partaking always forms the point of departure. "Nothing favors the view that Jesus regarded only the eating as important and that the reference to his death is a later addition. Conversely, however, it is also not probable that Jesus intended his action at the last meal to be only symbolical and that its connection with the meal arose only through external causes." Likewise the bread is not a mere symbol, but on the basis of the symbol the bread is at least a representative and mediator of the body of Jesus.

25   The moment of partaking and the moment of presentation are held together by the concept of the sacrificial meal. Because of their familiarity with Israel's world of religious concepts, Jesus' disciples knew and understood his thoughts. In the concept of the sacrificial meal the repetition was directly given, and likewise the reception of the gift given in the meal. Thus Jesus, in spite of the fact that we have no command of repetition, thought of a repetition, even according to Mark's account, because he gave a gift, which has value even for the most distant times.

As was the case for Erich Haupt, so also for Fr. Schultzen, eschatological conceptions are able to achieve only a secondary importance, since the repetition of the celebration is already firmly established in another way. "The thoughts of the parousia which are associated with this celebration are easily explained by the ardent desire of the Church for the parousia, since the Lord's Supper according to 1 Corinthians 11:26 is also a celebration which reaches its goal in the return of Christ."

The separation of the meal from the Lord's Supper is already presupposed for the primitive Church. Paul simply gave a strong emphasis to what was already there. The later separation of the "Eucharist" from the meal is much more simply explained if the Eucharist was already a special part of the meal than if that which was especially peculiar about it could not be recognized at all.

5. R. A. Hoffmann

Die Abendmahls Gedanken Jesu Christi. Königsberg, 1896.

[Richard Adolf Hoffmann (1872-1948), professor at Königsberg, is mentioned briefly in Schweitzer's *Geschichte der Leben-Jesu-Forschung*, p. 350, n.9; 354; n.11; p. 584, n.37, especially for modernizing Jesus. —J. R.]

For Hoffmann the moment of presentation is much more prominent than for Schultzen. Hoffmann actually presupposes two different kinds of participants. The action of presentation is meant for one kind, the participation for the other. "His blood was poured out for the unbelieving people; he gave it to drink to his own."

With the latter reference to drinking by his own, Hoffmann intends to say that, since the blood is the soul, Jesus' soul will flow over into them to give them power for their impending high mission, to strengthen them, so that they also, if the occasion should arise, will be able on their part to give their soul as a ransom for others. Jesus does not offer them his corpse but his living body as the bearer of the divine Spirit which dwells in him.

"In the primitive Christian celebration, besides the eating and drinking, also that which Jesus did, the breaking and giving thanks—in corresponding repetition—becomes significant." This was the viewpoint of Schultzen. Hoffmann goes still farther. "That which was essential about the first meal was not to be repeated without further ado, even the action of the Lord—how his over-towering spiritual greatness, his power, and his life-exuding presence yet for the final

26

time had proved itself to them in this action" (p. 106).

A repetition without a command of repetition is, therefore, unthinkable. The command of repetition must above all have referred to the partaking, since Jesus had instituted a meal in his memory. We can no longer determine how in the first period the Lord's Supper of the more intimate ones was related to the congregational meal. For Paul, in any case, the festive congregational meal was inseparably bound up with the Lord's Supper.

In Hoffmann's interpretation, eschatology is not significant.

Chapter VII

The Connection Between the Individual Questions and the Laws Which Govern It

1. The Command of Repetition

The historical celebration is a meal: its repetition is based upon the nature of the meal itself. If Jesus confers a special, somehow blessed significance upon the eating and drinking in the common circle of his own, then this action without further ado requires that the meal be repeated, and Jesus did not need to articulate this requirement as a command of repetition.

This is the viewpoint of the one-sided interpretations which stress exclusively the moment of partaking, and also of the two-sided interpretations which take the moment of partaking as their basis. If the disciples understood Jesus, they must of their own accord repeat this celebration. On the other hand, insofar as the moment of presentation is stressed along with the moment of partaking, the repetition is then not at all self-evident. That which Jesus did cannot really be repeated.

Thus these two-sided interpretations start with the thought that the command of repetition is actually superfluous, but then go on to suppose that it is nevertheless somehow possible or necessary.

27   The question for them, therefore, remains suspended in midair. The more strongly the idea of the passion and the moment of presentation are asserted to be important for the historical celebration, the greater the decisiveness with which a command of repetition is required in order to explain the ensuing repetition.

2. The Lord's Supper and the Primitive Christian Congregational Meal

There lies hidden in the congregational celebration a double aspect. A common meal is repeated. In doing so, however, a historical moment, unique in itself, is in some manner supposed to be reproduced. What is the relationship between the repeated "Lord's Meal" and the common religious meals of primitive Christianity?

According to the interpretations which one-sidedly develop the moment of partaking, both meals are identical, for these views hold that the historical celebration also consists only in the meal as such. The two-sided interpretations, however, get into the same difficulty here as with the command of repetition. They also, insofar as they take the character of the meals as their basis, should actually proclaim the identity of the two meals. But in addition to the moment of partaking, they also stress the moment of presentation, with the result that the congregational celebration becomes the repetition of a definite historical situation, which is no longer reproduced by the common meal as such. The repeated Lord's Meal should, therefore, now be somehow contrasted with the common religious meal, but only insofar as the final unity of both is maintained. The difficulty grows when a stronger emphasis is put upon the moment of presentation. The following scale results:

W. Brandt: Jesus makes the common meals the symbol of fellowship. When faith in him was newly revived after his death, the symbol of fellowship given by the Lord himself was naturally cherished to an unusual degree. The congregational meal and the "Lord's Meal" are identical.

Fr. Spitta: "Over bread and wine they always thought about how he had referred at that time to his being now and in all eternity the proper food and refreshment of their soul." The Didache represents the primitive Christian celebration. The Lord's Meal and the Agape were, according to the Didache, identical. It is incorrect to want to interpret Didache 9 and 10 as introductory prayers to the "actual celebration of the Lord's Supper."

Ad. Harnack: Here begins the differentiation. It is contained in the classical sentence with the "sidings": "The Lord instituted a memorial meal of his death, or rather, he designated (through the forgiveness of sins) the bodily food as his flesh and his blood, that is, as the food of the soul, if this food is partaken of with thanksgiving in memory of his death. Thus did the apostles understand his institution." A celebration, in which all of these finer meanings are supposed to be expressed, is however no longer a simple common meal but a ceremony. "Jesus promised them that he would be present with the power of his forgiveness of sins at each meal which they would observe in his memory." But how was the common meal designated as a "memorial meal"? Through which acts, through which words? How was the situation of the historical meal reproduced where also the "Lord's Supper" ("Abendmahl") had really been only a special moment in the course of the last common meal? 28

Erich Haupt: "The entire meeting is supposed to bear a religious character, and the Lord's Meal in the narrower sense is only the high point of the whole." Because Haupt stresses the moment of presentation more strongly than does Harnack, he cannot somehow let the congregational meal and the "Lord's Supper" ("Abendmahl") be merged together, but he must interpret the Lord's Supper as a special situation, which represents the high point of the entire meal-meeting. He cannot therefore avoid letting the "repeated action" (which is repeated on the basis of the institution) be set off from the religious meal and yet he cannot avoid maintaining anew the final unity of both. Thus there remains for him only the relationship of intensification.

Spitta and Harnack deny that in Didache 10:6 ("if any is holy, let him come") a special celebration begins. As for Haupt, he must find his intensification here again, and he assumes that these words introduce the actual celebration of the Lord's Supper. The words, "Lord, come!," refer to the presence of the Lord in the "sacrament."

Fr. Schultzen: By means of the concept of the "sacrificial meal" Schultzen holds the two competitive parts of the celebration together. No longer, however, can he, like Erich Haupt, place them in the relationship of intensification—his stress on the moment of presentation is already much too strong for that—but he must confirm the 29 separation. "The repetition of the meal is directly given in the concept of the sacrificial meal and likewise the regular reception of the gift which is distributed" (p. 74). But in the second place the action of the Institutor of the sacrificial meal is repeated, as the presupposition of the reception and of the partaking by the participants. "The gift which he bestows upon them was supposed to have the result, and also actually did have the result, that they repeated what he had done, and in doing so they also shared more fully in the blessing of his sacrificial death" (p. 96).

But how can we conceive that the disciples at a common meal "repeated what he had done"? That means nothing else but that the congregational meal and the Lord's Supper were intended to be separated. In 1 Corinthians 11 Paul only emphasizes more strongly the separation for which the way was already prepared before him. The fact that afterwards the Eucharist was completely detached from the meal "is only the historical consummation of the process which was already contained in the institution."

R. A. Hoffmann: The moment of presentation stands out so prominently that Hoffmann gives up hope of solving the problem. "That which was essential about the first celebration of the Lord's Supper was not to be repeated without further ado, even the action of the Lord" (p. 106). The command of repetition cannot refer to the action performed by Jesus himself. But to refer this command to the action of the participants, the eating and the drinking, is, to be sure, grammatically impossible, so to say. But since we have no other alternative, we must certainly suppose that Jesus, as a means of perserving his memory, "instituted a meal."

How Jesus wanted that to be understood is not clear. We must seriously reckon with the possibility "that that which has been transmitted to us from Jesus' words at the institution of his meal does not represent everything which he actually spoke to clarify his action, an action which for us today is so difficult to understand" (p. 115).

We cannot attain complete clarity about how the celebration was observed in primitive Christianity. We know only "that the Lord's Supper in the primitive Church was an actual meal at which it is very probable that the breaking of bread was simultaneously the Lord's Meal" (p. 137).

Summary. Our investigation results in the following proposition: when the moment of participation is stressed exclusively, the congre-

30

gational meal and the Lord's Supper are identical. When the moment of presentation is stressed as of secondary importance, it becomes necessary to differentiate between the two meals to an increasing degree, until finally the two are separated.

3. The Antinomy between the Historical and the Primitive Christian Celebrations

Probably not the least service of Spitta's splendid study is that it proclaims with utter sharpness the principle that an interpretation of the Lord's Supper has value only if it clarifies the essence of the primitive Christian celebration as we find it especially in the Didache. Accordingly, the primitive Christian celebration also forms the chief support of his interpretation. He does perfect justice to the primitive Christian celebration, since according to his interpretation the Lord's Meal was a joyful meal. Since he abandons a command of repetition and a separation of the "Lord's Supper" from the congregational meal, he agrees completely with the primitive Christian tradition. This tradition, of course, also knows nothing about the idea that the celebration was supposed to be an avowed reproduction of that historical situation, a reproduction which ensued upon Jesus' command.

Whereas Spitta thus completely explains the primitive Christian celebration, he can in no way even begin to do justice to the historical celebration. This failure he shares with all interpretations which one-sidedly develop the moment of partaking. To what extent the disciples must have understood and did understand Jesus as he invited them to partake of his body and blood: in no way are Spitta and company able, without forbidden artifices, to make that plain. So far as the historical situation is concerned, they have nothing left but skepticism, whereby they may find consolation in the fact that they at least are doing justice to the primitive Christian celebration.

As for the two-sided interpretations, the situation is as follows: the more they stress the moment of presentation, the better and more plausibly they are able to explain the historical celebration, since they now can utilize the idea of the passion and the symbolism of Jesus' action to interpret the figurative sayings. To the same extent, however, they become incapable of explaining the primitive Christian celebration. Indeed, with the moment of presentation is given the command of repetition, the significance of the idea of the passion for the celebration, and the differentiation between the Lord's Supper and the con-

31

gregational meal. The primitive Christian tradition, however, is diametrically opposed to all of that. This tradition knows nothing of that, but limits itself in a remarkable way to the proposition: the Lord's Supper is a joyous meal, during which Jesus' act of presentation is not reproduced in any way.

The antinomy is, therefore, insoluble. A two-sided interpretation explains the historical celebration only to the extent that it does not explain the primitive Christian celebration and vice versa. This proposition contains the basic result of our investigation of the two-sided interpretations. Consequently they must forego the solution of the problem, since none of them, be they ever so ingenious, can overcome this antinomy.

This antinomy is grounded precisely in the previous formulation of the problem itself. This formulation wants to interpret the primitive Christian celebration as an appropriate repetition of the historical celebration. However, that which is repeated is, because of history, not at all similar to the original. The historical celebration is a ceremony during the course of a meal. The primitive Christian celebration is only a common meal without an appropriate repetition of the ceremony. With this state of affairs the antimony is inescapably given.

It is, however, an established fact that the primitive Christian celebration goes back to the historical celebration. Therefore the problem is solved only when the connection of the two celebrations is explained, but this does not mean that the congregational celebration is somehow an appropriate imitation of the historical celebration. The primitive Christian celebration of the Lord's Supper is something independent in its own right.

Chapter VIII

The Interpretations
with a One-Sided Stress
upon the Moment of Presentation

1. The Field of Battle

The interpretations with exclusive emphasis upon the moment of partaking indicated a daring rejection of the widespread interpretation which is represented by the names of Rückert, Holtzmann, and Lobstein. It could appear for a moment as if the conventional view had lost all its positions through this unexpected, united attack against the explanation of the figurative sayings on the basis of Jesus' action. Now, however, where the situation slowly becomes clear, it becomes evident that this is not the case.

Indeed, several exposed positions had to be given up by the part attacked. Accordingly, this part withdrew to a position which may be regarded as invincible. As matters stand, the attacker of this fortified position must reject the thought of ever conquering it. The defender, however, cannot for some time consider an action in the open field.

Among the positions given up belongs above all that regarding the question of the Passover meal. Whereas until the seventies and eighties the last meal was almost universally regarded as a Passover meal, in accordance with the Synoptics, the attempt is now made to remove this question from its connection with the total conception. Scholars are content to make a cautious examination of the chronology involved to see whether or not the Synoptic date is probable.

The situation is similar in respect to the command of repetition. Even the interpretations which take the moment of presentation as their basis are seeking to free themselves from the necessity of a saying which refers to the repetition.

At the same time, the moment of partaking is on the whole accentuated much more decisively than was previously the case. It nevertheless always remains dependent upon, and becomes understandable only through, the moment of presentation.

These shifts in position can best be pursued in the successive publications of Lobstein and Holtzmann, insofar as they are concerned with the question of the Lord's Supper. They have prepared the defense position.

2. The Defense Plan: P. W. Schmiedel

"Die neuesten Ansichten über den Ursprung des Abendmahls," *Protestantische Monatshefte*, 1899.

[For P. W. Schmiedel, see above, pp. 68-69, where Schweitzer referred to him as "Wilhelm Schmiedel." —J. R.]

In opposition to the rather robust procedure of Eichhorn, Schmiedel undertook to set forth the actual state of affairs. He shows, first of all, that as a whole the chronological arguments against the possibility that the last meal was a Passover meal are certainly very impressive. If, however, we examine them one after the other, they suffer a significant loss of energy. The supposition that Jesus celebrated the legal Passover is therefore not to be rejected out of hand, since the straightforward statements of the Synoptics are well able to counterbalance the chronological objections.

Moreover, the idea of the Passover may be drawn on, in an appropriate way, to explain the historical celebration, whereby the possibility is to be reckoned with that in Jesus' mind Passover and Covenant ideas flowed together.

So far as the action which Jesus is supposed to have undertaken is concerned, it is to be supposed that the significant aspect, at least primarily, is the breaking of the bread and the pouring of the wine out of the pitcher into the cup. The distribution of these foods to partake of follows as a matter of secondary importance. "So far as the main point was concerned, this distribution and partaking would not have been necessary, but since the participants formerly sat at the meal [in contrast to our present practices], it was natural." On the whole it serves the same purpose as the meal following a covenant sacrifice or the Passover sacrifice, that is, the purpose of the common appropriation and nurturing of the thoughts which occur during the sacrifice.

For Schmiedel, the question whether the command of repetition is historical or not, remains suspended in midair, If we were certain that it had been handed down, then it would be understandable. But it is likewise comprehensible that Jesus did not think of a repetition.

In respect to ingenious recklessness, calm consideration is absolutely necessary. P. 148: "We must call your attention to the urgency with which we advise you to approach with a positive attitude each attempt similar to ours, if you want to avoid insoluble difficulties." The great value of Schmiedel's position is, of course, due to the support which it finds in a natural exegesis of our New Testament accounts of the Lord's Supper. By emphasizing the moment of presentation, Schmiedel can accommodate in his total interpretation every single feature of the historical situation, every secondary thought indicated by exegesis. He has succeeded in raising to a very high degree of probability "the possibility that Jesus really administered a celebration which corresponds approximately to the discription." The derivation of the accounts from the later theology of the church, perhaps 34 even by utilizing non-Christian analogies, becomes meaningless of itself. Every construction of this sort must first produce the proof that the alleged transformation could have come into use in such a short time after Jesus' death.

But with that effort the value of this defensive position has exhausted itself. It has at its disposal sure-fire, well-placed cannon, which however do not carry very far, so that before the eyes of the beleaguered, the swarms of besieging cavalrymen enjoy themselves and exercise undisturbed on the undisputed terrain. It is, of course, impossible that an interpretation related to Schmiedel's could ever explain how the historical celebration, which is understood in detail by such interpretations, was repeated in primitive Christianity, especially without the assumption of a command of Jesus referring to such repetition. For Schmiedel and those who share his viewpoint, the emphasis, of course, lies in Jesus' action. Now this action of Jesus was not repeated at all in the primitive Christian celebration, because such a repetition is impossible. The idea of the passion is, of course, totally missing from the primitive celebration. It is a meal at which, so far as we know, the ceremony of the historical celebration was in no way reproduced. The secondary matter, the eating, has therefore become the chief matter, and the chief matter has completely disappeared from the repeated celebration.

Outside of the narrow sector which is controlled by the cannon of the fortress, the smallest band of attacking cavalrymen has the advantage against the well-armed but cumbersome garrison, if it should dare to attack. Every bold construction, from Strauss to Eichhorn, can better explain the rise and the essence of the primitive Christian celebration than can Schmiedel's exegetically scrupulous interpretation, which is distilled from the accounts. Only let the former keep itself out of range of the exegetical defensive fire, if it does not want to be put out of action by the first shot. A remarkable battle indeed, where no one is surprised that each acts as victor, even though the other is unconquered.

3. The Offensive: Adolf Jülicher

Zur Geschichte der Abendmahlsfeier in der ältesten Kirche, 1892. "Theologische Abhandlungen," dedicated to K. von Weizsäcker.

[Best known for his work on the parables and for a New Testament introduction, Adolf Jülicher (1857-1938) was professor of Church History and New Testament at Marburg. Cf. Schweitzer's *Quest,* pp. 242, 263-65, among other references. — J. R.]

Jülicher is most nearly in accord with Zwingli, whose interpretation he modernizes by taking into consideration the modern form of the questions. It is a matter of a one-sided stress on the moment of presentation.

All interpretations which are based upon the moment of partaking attribute modern conceptions to Jesus. What he said at that meal for the last time with such unusual solemnity must have been directly understandable to each one present. The point of comparison must therefore lie in that which he does before the eyes of the disciples with the elements to be partaken of: in the breaking of bread and in the pouring out of the wine. The meaning of the accompanying words refer to his impending death. " 'Just as this wine will immediately disappear, so immediately will my blood be poured out, for my death is a foregone conclusion; but,' he adds assuringly, 'it will not be poured out in vain, but "for many" and'—a figurative expression which lay in the circle of ideas associated with Passover day—'as blood of the covenant'." Jesus here and there compares only the object of the partaking with his body—he does not reflect at all upon the act of partaking. Insofar as the moment of partaking receives any kind of meaning from the preceding moment of presentation, we can at the most concede to it problematic importance. Thus the celebration originally had a sad, painful character, which can be understood only in context.

Now the oldest tradition does not let Jesus indicate in any way that he desired to see that meaningful action also carried out in the future by those who believe in him. But how then was the primitive church so quickly able to make out of this historical celebration a definite action to be repeated regularly? At first it was probably an inner need. Passover ideas and memories of farewell worked together. Soon the repetition occurred in connection with every meal, and there arose the conception of an express command of Jesus referring to repetition. "So far as possible, they wanted to reproduce the original situation, except that now they looked back to that which at that time was supposed to be proclaimed" (p. 247). This celebration was named, in shortened form, after the first act, the breaking of bread. In connection with the distribution of the sacramental elements, believers probably did not from time immemorial repeat verbatim the Lord's words of institution with their respective meanings, for otherwise their transmission would not show so many differences. According to 1 Corinthians 11:26, no one had ever neglected, in connection with the distribution, to proclaim the Lord's death, and therefore again and again to place that shocking event before their eyes, and to discuss its necessity as well as it blessed effects. But all this was done freely and not according to set forms.

4. Skepticism in the Interpretations with a One-Sided Stress upon the Moment of Presentation

Jülicher's study means for the interpretations of the Lord's Supper which in a thoroughgoing manner take the moment of presentation as their basis, what Eichhorn's essay means for the interpretations which take the moment of partaking as their basis. Both show by the consequence of their thought-structure that their sole stress upon the moment which they take as their basis necessarily leads to skepticism. The results come to light in the case of Eichhorn in that he was not able to explain the historical celebration when he viewed it from the perspective of the primitive Christian congregational celebration. Jülicher cannot explain the congregational celebration from the vantage point of the historical celebration.

Jülicher is altogether correct when he says that those interpretations which take as their basis the moment of partaking require the help of modern ideas to explain the historical sayings of Jesus. But is it not likewise transferring very modern ideas into bygone times if someone wants to make comprehensible the primitive Christian celebration as the intentional reproduction, as exact as possible, of the original situation? Jülicher's interpretation could explain the Zwinglian congregational celebration (and yet Jülicher lacks the command of repetition) but never the primitive Christian religious congregational meal.

The difficulties are developed with absolute clarity precisely through his sharp and logically unified overall interpretation. He does not allow himself to distinguish between the Lord's Supper in the actual sense and the congregational meal. All varieties of the two-sided presentations had operated with this latitude, and by so doing they had overcome the greatest difficulties. The entire congregational celebration is "the Lord's Meal"—so says Jülicher, and in so saying he agrees with no one so completely as with Spitta and Eichhorn.

As a result, however, the antinomy which leads to skepticism is necessarily given. The congregational celebration to which Jülicher comes from his understanding of the historical celebration is a fiction which directly contradicts the actual primitive Christian meal celebration, since the latter was "no reproduction of the original situation." He can in no wise show how the repetition arose. "At first it was probably an inner need, with which Passover ideas and memories of farewell worked together": this problematic and twisted supposition explains nothing at all about the repetition.

Now Jülicher could have gotten around the difficulty by means of the command of repetition, but his exegetical conscience did not permit him to take this way out. Although he absolutely needed this command, he did not lay claim to it because it is not attested by the two oldest Synoptics. His attractive interpretation grew out of his exegetical examination of the accounts. But it is precisely his exegesis which deprives him of the only possibility of making comprehensible even in some degree the repetition in primitive Christianity of the celebration described by him. The primitive Christian celebration as a reproduction of the historical situation without a command of repetition is simply inconceivable. Therefore we are here standing before a complete self-dissolution. In order to explain the rise of the primitive Christian celebration, Jülicher had to postulate a fact which is given independently of the accounts—as does Eichhorn, in order to make the rise of the historical account comprehensible.

The thoroughgoing stress upon the moment of presentation leads, therefore, to the same skepticism as does the one-sided development of the moment of partaking.

Chapter IX
The New Formulation of the Problem

1. The Result of the Investigation

The interpretations with a one-sided emphasis upon the moment of partaking can explain only the primitive Christian celebration, never the historical celebration.

The interpretations with a one-sided emphasis upon the moment of presentation can explain only the historical celebration, never the primitive Christian celebration.

The two-sided interpretations can explain the historical celebration only to the extent that they do not explain the primitive Christian celebration, and vice versa.

Therefore none of these interpretations is able to solve the problem of the Lord's Supper, since this problem plainly requires that both celebrations be understood in their mutual relationship!

These propositions apply not only to the interpretations which have been especially analyzed here, for these interpretations are only types of many others which have already been published or are still slumbering in the womb of time. Past or future, all interpretations are brought to a preliminary trial and quickly disposed of by the above three propositions. Before interpretations can be heard at all, they must first prove that they are something other than a new combination of the moments of presentation and partaking. If they cannot do that, they are rejected in advance, for they are not able to solve the problem. It is not a matter of their specific character or of the manner in which they are presented, historically and exegetically, but it is only a matter of the relationship between the moment of presentation and the moment of partaking in these interpretations. Everything else is of secondary importance.

Every interpretation is conditioned by the formula which expresses the relation assumed by it of the moment of presentation to the moment of partaking. That is what really decides its attitude toward the individual questions—the command of repetition, the meaning of the figurative sayings, the form of the supposed primitive Christian celebration, etc. Each interpretation can at once be evaluated according to this basic formula. Whatever the authors then add in the way of flashes of inspiration, exegetical discoveries, and ingenious inconsistencies—that is all of no consequence. Without their realizing it, they are really following an inner compulsion. Because they must, they take on the most difficult exegetical obstacles. Because they cannot do otherwise, they overlook the weighty historical questions! Because they may sketch the flourishes on the balcony to suit themselves, they are—and the others with them—inclined to forget that they have abandoned the ground plan of the building.

Under the given presuppositions, there are no more new interpretations of the Lord's Supper. Whether an interpretation grows out of an exegetical or historical observation, it can basically be nothing other than the repetition or modification of an interpretation already in existence, that is, an interpretation with which it has in common the formula setting forth the relationship of the two moments. If someone wanted to take the pains to draw up the family tree of the existing interpretations, it would not be difficult to discover the ancestors of each interpretation.

The interpretations with a one-sided development of the moment of partaking are only the scholarly-historical reproduction of the old Greek interpretation.

Zwingli rationalized the Roman theory, and he was transposed by Jülicher into a modern-historical key.

The two-sided interpretations repeat in historical form the attempts to mediate between the Mass and the Greek Mystery and those of the Reformation period. We can therefore say without hesitation that all possible combinations of the two moments have been exhausted.

Therefore nothing is accomplished by "new interpretations." The new in them is always the burst of inspiration, never the formula—and everything depends upon the latter. Thus the dispute about the details of such a new interpretation leads to absolutely nothing. That which is found to be "right" and that which is found to be "false" are connected according to the law: one is right only insofar as the other is false.

For that reason works of the kind which Rud. Schäfer, Clemen,[1] and Schmiedel have contributed to the most recent discussions do not, in spite of all their conscientiousness, advance research in proportion to the ingenuity expended. On the basis of that which they recognize, no new interpretations can be built up, and that which they have to offer does not suffice to overthrow the other interpretations, if there is nothing better to put in their place.

Those who under the given circumstances draw up new interpretations of the Lord's Supper are doing over and over a problem in division which has always refused to come out even. Their critics do the problem again and again, but they still can not make it come out even.

It can never come out even. Therefore it profits nothing always to start afresh with zeal and concentration. The error must be sought, not in the calculation, but at the outset. The previous interpretations do not get beyond dialectical assertions, which as a whole cannot be proved or refuted on the basis of historical facts.

Let us therefore free ourselves from the previous formulation of the problem.

Where does the basis of the metaphysical lie in the question of the Lord's Supper?

40

---

[1] *Der Ursprung des heil. Abendmahls,* by Lic. Dr. Karl Clemen, 1898. "Hefte zur christl. Welt," no. 37.

2. The New Way

Previously this proposition was considered to be valid: in order to explain the Lord's Supper, one must begin with the meaning of the figurative sayings, for these constitute the essence of the celebration. Therefore scholars sought to interpret the figurative sayings on the basis of the partaking, or of the action, or of both together—and if they found a plausible explanation, they believed they possessed the key to the Lord's Supper.

Now, however, it is a matter of opening two doors: but the key in question fits only one door at a time. Granted that Spitta and the others interpret the figurative sayings correctly in respect to primitive Christianity: the historical situation, however, does not correspond to their explanation. Granted that Jülicher and the others interpret the figurative sayings correctly on the basis of the historical situation: but their explanation is not in the sense of primitive Christianity, for there the idea is in no way expressed that the action of Jesus symbolized his death.

We have every reason to ask, however, whether the figurative sayings are explainable without further ado on the basis of the action which accompanies them. Indeed, all explanations are reached in a roundabout way! How is the breaking of bread supposed to indicate the crucifixion of the body? Is this explanation, therefore, perhaps more illuminating because it is the only one which leaves the accompanying action open? Who says to us that the disciples could have understood it in this way? In the primitive Christian and early Christian eras, indeed, actually until Zwingli, no one knew anything of this explanation.

Matters are even worse when it comes to the saying over the cup. Here scholars must, if they want to make sense out of the figurative saying, actually invent the action to be compared. Only the passing around of the cup is reported. But this action does not characterize the "pouring out of the blood." The only tolerable comparison would be the "pouring out into the cup." Now even though this action is not mentioned in any account, all exegetical interpretations, which are based upon the moment of presentation, have to do with the "pouring out" of the wine into the cup. Out of an inner necessity they freely create an analogy to the breaking of the bread, but they are unable to defend the procedure whereby they enrich the situation in a prohibited way.

Where, then, does it stand written that Jesus meaningfully poured the wine into the cup before the eyes of the disciples, or how he broke the bread? Nowhere! Therefore the exegetical interpretation of the second figurative saying is based on pure invention.

Let us confess it openly: we have no guide to a natural interpretation of the figurative sayings. As a result, we have not been able to get beyond artificiality. Our key is only a poor master key: in emergency it fits one lock, but not both. And on the basis of this makeshift explanation of the figurative sayings we want to explain the entire historical and primitive Christian meal celebration!

If in this emergency we would focus our attention for just a moment upon the only possible way out! It will not do to explain the celebration by means of the figurative sayings. Let us try it with the opposite procedure, namely, to explain the figurative sayings on the basis of the celebration!

It is true that at first this procedure appears to be the last desperate shaking of the locked door. But let us calmly consider the matter for a moment.

At the Lord's Supper it is a matter of the distribution on Jesus' part, of the participation on the disciples' part, and of two figurative sayings, which coincide with the procedure. I say "coincide"! In a situation, actions and speeches can coincide chronologically, whereas in the account they can be portrayed only in chronological succession, because the sayings necessarily explain each simultaneity as a succession.

Thus our accounts contain the sequence: distribution, figurative saying, partaking, as if Jesus had first acted symbolically, then distributed, and then spoken the explanatory figurative saying, after which the disciples ate with understanding.

But if we for a moment try to conceive of the reported procedure as a scene, then we shall soon notice that the neat chronological order becomes quite illusory. Let us picture twelve men, who, as if by an agreement among themselves, wait to eat the piece shared with them until Jesus has spoken the figurative saying. How unnatural, indeed, impossible, this scene is in the aforesaid chronological order of the actions, can be seen when it is translated into life at Oberammergau! It is almost impossible to think of anything more unnatural and stilted.

For anyone who is able to visualize a reported situation with an artist's eye for reality, there remain only two possibilities. Either Jesus

42

distributed the bread to each individual, and as he did so repeated the figurative saying for each individual: in this way the chronological order is tenable. Or, as is certain, he distributed bread to all of them together and spoke the figurative saying only once: then the chronological order with which we previously operated becomes illusory. After all, our accounts say only that Jesus spoke the figurative sayings about body and blood during the course of distributing the bread and during the passing around of the cup! Whether at the beginning, in the middle, or at the end; whether before, during, or after the eating and drinking—that cannot be determined. Our accounts give no particulars about this matter.

Out of the supposed chronological order the previous interpretations have without further ado made a causal sequence. It was said: the distribution and the preceding breaking and pouring provide the foundation for the figurative saying; the figurative saying is supposed to explain the meaning of the partaking to the disciples; and the meaning of the partaking constitutes the essence of the celebration.

To make a causal sequence out of a supposed chronological order is a mistake which human thought makes again and again, in spite of all warnings, and in doing so creates the greatest problems for itself.

Now history shows that precisely this supposed causal sequence makes the problem of the Lord's Supper insolvable. On the other hand, our knowledge of the situation is restricted to the fact that Jesus during the course of the distribution spoke the figurative sayings. Therefore let us free ourselves from the prejudice that the figurative sayings constituted the celebration, and let us so conceive the problem that the celebration explains the figurative sayings. In other words: it was previously thought that Jesus invited the disciples to partake of the bread which he offered and of the wine which he passed around, 43 because he had designated these elements as his body and his blood (but in this case no one can say with certainty in what sense the disciples, with bread and wine, ate and drank his body and his blood).

We proceed, however, upon the basis that Jesus says of the bread and the wine (which his disciples partake of when he offers it to them), "This is my body," and "This is my blood," precisely in view of the fact that they partake of it when he offers it! They, therefore, do not eat his body and drink his blood, but, because they eat that bread and drink that wine, he says it is his body and his blood! The figurative saying, then, does not constitute the celebration, but it grows out of it.

The celebration is independent! It consists of the fact that Jesus with thanksgiving breaks the bread for his disciples and passes around the cup and they partake of it. The figurative sayings do not belong to the essence of the celebration, but Jesus expresses in these mysterious sayings the meaning which the celebration has for him!

The second possibility is as plainly found in the accounts as is the first. Scholars have always overlooked this alternative, however, because the chronological order of the actions in the literary representation captured all their attention for the first possibility.

Now, however, it is logically established that the previous supposition makes the problem completely insoluble. Therefore we must of necessity attempt to solve it with the second supposition.

Moreover, history plainly supports the second supposition. It is certain that the figurative passion sayings played no role in the primitive Christian celebration. They were in no way reproduced in the course of the celebration. This contention is supported by the Didache and Paul, for if these sayings had been known from the daily course of the celebration, then 1 Corinthians 11:23 would remain incomprehensible, for here then something known would be repeated in a secretive way! Therefore the matter stood like this in primitive Christianity: it was well-known that these figurative sayings had been spoken at the historical celebration; the congregational celebration was derived from this historical celebration; but still in doing so no one felt any need to reproduce the historical figurative sayings of Jesus in any way. Hence the historical celebration was, insofar as it was continued in the congregational celebration, independent of the figurative sayings, since otherwise the figurative sayings would also have been repeated. 4 That is attested by history.

Therefore the problem of the Lord's Supper no longer has anything at all to do with the two impossible questions: How did Jesus give his disciples his body to eat and his blood to drink? And how did they later reproduce this celebration in an appropriate way? Now the problem itself is entirely different. It is no more: what is the meaning of the figurative sayings so that we can explain the celebration? but what does the celebration mean so that we can explain the figurative sayings?

In what sense was the distribution of bread and wine at the last meal such an extremely solemn act which referred to Jesus' death? The investigation must commence with this question, because from the first it completely leaves the figurative sayings aside. It is the only way to the solution of the problem.

Part Two

The Problem of the Lord's Supper according to the Historical Accounts

Abbreviations

Manuscripts and Ancient Versions
of the New Testament cited by Schweitzer*

Greek uncial manuscripts

SYMBOL	NAME	DATE	LOCATION	NUMBER
ℵ	Sinaiticus	4th cent.	London, British Museum	01[1]
A	Alexandrinus	5th cent.	London, British Museum	02
B	Vaticanus	4th cent.	Rome, Vatican	03
C	Ephraemi Rescriptus	5th cent.	Paris, Biblio. Nat.	04
D	Beza	5th or 6th cent.	Cambridge Univ. Lib.	05
E		8th cent.	Basle, Univ. Lib.	07
F		9th cent.	Utrecht	09
H		9th cent. or later	Hamburg, Cambridge	013
L	Regius	8th cent.	Paris, Biblio. Nat.	019
M[3]		9th cent.	Paris, Biblio. Nat.	021[2]
Γ		10th cent.	Oxford, Bodleian Lib.	036
Δ		9th cent.	St. Gall	037
Z		6th cent.	Dublin, Trinity College	035

Old Latin manuscripts

a	4th cent.	Vercelli	3
b	5th cent.	Verona	4
c	12-13th cent.	Paris, Biblio. Nat.	6
ff[2]	5th cent.	Paris, Biblio. Nat.	8

Syriac

syr [cu]	Curetonian Syriac manuscript	5th cent.

Westcott and Hort, edition of the Greek New Testament, 1881

---

*Editor's note.—J.R.

[1]a = first corrector's hand

[2]3 = third corrector's hand

Chapter X

The Questions Raised by Textual Criticism

1. Codex D. The Chief Question Raised by Textual Criticism

The matter in question is the Lucan account (Luke 22:15-20). In the usual form this account has a peculiar character. It begins with a saying about eating the Passover in the future kingdom. There follows a similar saying concerning the cup, a saying which corresponds to the concluding eschatological saying of the Synoptics, according to Mark and Matthew. After this first "little discourse" on the eating and drinking is concluded, there comes the saying about the broken bread and about the wine as the blood of the covenant. Thus the concluding eschatological saying, which in the two earlier Synoptics follows the covenant-saying and concludes the second act, is missing from Luke at this point.

We have, therefore, a remarkable duality: two sayings concerning the eating and two concerning the cup. Of the two sayings which refer to the eating, only the second has to do with the partaking of the bread, whereas the first speaks about the Passover in general. The duality here is therefore not so striking as it is with the two sayings concerning the drinking, both of which refer to the cup. The second saying looks like a supplement to the first: it appears without the concluding eschatological saying, it does not contain the invitation to partake, and in this form it does not at all provide a conclusion which rounds off the celebration, as does the old Synoptic cup-saying.

Since this peculiar duality in the Lucan account was so striking, therefore, the most natural correction was already given: to delete the second cup-saying—since the invitation to partake seemed to be contained already in the first—but on the other hand to let stand the second saying over the bread (the bread was not previously mentioned in its specific character), because it contains the invitation to partake. This is the correction of Codex D.[1] It concludes with the words: τοῦτό ἐστι τὸ σῶμά μου (verse 19a).

If we once opt for this deletion which is so natural, then there remains no more reason at all to allow the cup-saying with its invitation to drink to force its way between the two statements referring to eating and to split them asunder unnaturally. Then we modulate back into the original Synoptic harmony, so that the concluding eschatological saying again comes at the end. If accordingly verses 17 and 18 then follow after 19a, then we have before us an account which is differentiated from the usual account only insofar as it has a Passover saying before the bread-saying, the Passover-saying being fashioned after the concluding eschatological saying over the cup. This procedure is followed by b and c.[2]

The origin of Codex D's account of the Lord's Supper is based on reflection. The conviction is generally gaining more and more ground that D's variations are of this nature throughout. This form of the narrative has no original conception of the historical celebration. Therefore the basic question about the Lucan form of the text is not at all concerned with Codex D but with the usual reading. How does it come about that Luke so lets the account be reflected as a duality that the attempt to correct this duality as going back to an error must necessarily appear in Codex D? This question, however, is no longer a

---

[1]D, a, ff². Westcott and Hort adopted this reading.

[2]For the same reason, syr^cu omits verse 20 and substitutes verses 17 and 18 for it.

problem of textual criticism at all, but it is bound up with the development of the celebration in primitive Christianity and the displacement during the course of that development of the picture of the historical meal.[3]

2. Variant Readings

47

The question as to whether in individual cases εὐλογήσας or εὐχαριστήσας is the correct reading has no significance. The two earlier Gospels employ the former expression; Paul, Luke, and Justin, the latter.

The reason for the various readings in Matthew 26:26 is easy to understand. Participles and finite verbs are heaped up here in such a manner that we can in no case avoid a cumbersome and un-Greek-like construction. Whether we now read: λαβὼν ὁ'Ιησοῦς ἄρτον καὶ εὐλογήσας ἔκλασεν καὶ δοὺς τοῖς μαθηταῖς εἶπεν,[4] or whether we resolve one of the participles and preserve the reading λαβὼν ὁ Ιησοῦς ἄρτον καὶ εὐλογήσας ἔκλασεν καὶ ἐδίδου τοῖς μαθηταῖς καὶ εἶπεν[5] makes no difference. In either case the sentence is formless, because it contains an abundance of actions for one moment, whose temporal and logical connections simply cannot be expressed linguistically. The variants are due to the difficulty experienced in trying to represent these actions, a difficulty which each scribe tried to overcome in a different way.

In Mark the stylistic difficulties are not so conspicuous. In particular he avoids naming the giver and the receivers, whereby the Matthean construction becomes so unusually awkward.

The Pauline and the Justinian accounts are free from this difficulty: they simplify the situation by omitting the presentation (ἔδωκεν) and the invitation to partake (λάβετε).

The φάγετε in Mark 14:22[6] is a naive imitation of Matthew. The early witnesses offer only λάβετε.

The addition καινῆς, which several variants offer with the saying

---

[3]A thorough exposition of the textual problems of the Lukan account is found in Erich Haupt's study.

[4]So ℵ (but ℵ[a] reads ἐδίδου instead of δούς BDLZ.

[5]ΑΓΔ.

[6]Mark 14:22: EFHM[3] add φάγετε after λάβετε.

over the cup in Mark 14:24,[7] is due to a naive imitation of the Pauline version.

3. The Result of Textual Criticism

The variety of readings is not based on the fact that one reading with its roots reaches higher up historically than the others. In part these variations result from the difficulty which the interpretations in question have in expressing themselves stylistically. In part they originate in the tendency to harmonize the accounts with each other. But for this purpose it was already too late: the various types had already received too sharp a historical stamp for the attempts at emendation to be able to succeed in restoring the uniform textual type, at which the preceding historical periods had worked so hard in vain.

The *textus receptus* offers the last attempt at this harmonization, inasmuch as it represents the first act according to Paul after the analogy with the Matthean account, and in so doing interpolates the invitation to partake (take, eat), which originally was missing from 1 Corinthians 11:24.

The task of textual criticism in the problem of the Lord's Supper consists in representing each of the accounts in its characteristic peculiarity by freeing each account from the traces of the attempted literary harmonization with the others. This task, as modest as it seems, is of the utmost importance. If the harmonization of the accounts had really succeeded, the problem of the Lord's Supper would be insolvable.

---

[7]Mark 14:24: τῆς διαθήκης (ℵ BCDL).

Chapter XI

48

The Peculiarity of the Marcan Account
(Mark 14:22-26)

The first act consists solely of Jesus' praying, breaking bread, and passing it around. At the same time, he utters the figurative saying about his body. There is missing from Mark, as from Matthew, the ὑπὲρ ὑμῶν, to which we are accustomed from Paul. On the other hand, Mark does not have Matthew's φάγετε.

If in the first act the invitation to partake is thus not expressly spoken in connection with the figurative saying, then from the second act the invitation is missing altogether. It is reported first that Jesus, after the word of prayer, passed the cup around to all and they all drank out of it (Mark 14:23). Only after that does he speak the figurative saying about the blood poured out for many (Mark 14:24).

To the best of my knowledge, Bruno Bauer was the first to point out that Mark, instead of reporting the invitation to drink, confirms that all have drunk. Bauer sees in this change only a toning down of Matthew, since Mark hesitated to preserve Jesus' invitation in its entirety.

But in so doing Bauer failed to notice that with this confirmation the usual chronological order from figurative saying to partaking is also disrupted, whereby at the same time the causal relationship, with which we are familiar, between figurative saying and participation is abolished. According to the Marcan account it is impossible for Jesus or the disciples to derive the meaning of the drinking from the figurative saying, because this saying follows only after the drinking!

We further observe how the concluding eschatological saying about drinking the wine new in the kingdom of the Father is spoken solemnly (ἀμήν) and emphatically and follows closely upon the figurative saying! It forms the high point of the celebration (verse 25), after which the departure follows immediately.

These peculiar features of the Marcan account have previously not been developed. Scholars have simply interpreted the Markan account according to the other accounts. Scholars assumed without further ado that all accounts offer the same data. At the last meal Jesus so offered the disciples bread and wine that they somehow ate and drank the elements as his body and his blood. Scholars explained the lack of the φάγετε in Mark by saying it was understood as a matter of course. They did not even accentuate the peculiarity of the second act because they interpreted it—without defending their procedure—according to Matthew and the other accounts.

The supposition that the Marcan account says essentially the same thing as the others is one of the unproved presuppositions with which the previous interpretations of the Lord's Supper operated. That is to say, if we had only the Marcan account no one would have thought that Jesus distributed to his disciples bread and wine as his body and his blood and invited them to partake in this sense. Scholars would interpret the chronological sequence of the first act according to that of the second act and establish as a fact that Jesus during the course of the distribution of the bread spoke the figurative saying about his body and after the passing around of the cup spoke the figurative saying about his blood. But if we have one account where Jesus, according to the strict wording of the text, distributed neither his body nor his blood to partake of, then we must not interpret this account according to the others, as if it were a matter of a certain carelessness and economy in expression, but we must compare this account with the others and create a controversy, which will then reveal the significance of the variations. Either it is a matter of an absolutely incomprehensible

50

portrayal, which as a curiosity we need to consider no further, because it has absolutely no relationship with the established state of affairs, or we have before us the authentic acount with which the investigation must begin. The moment that we clearly recognize the peculiarity of the Marcan account we cannot avoid this alternative.

Chapter XII
The Comparison of the Accounts

1. The Principle of Harmonization

Externally considered, the peculiarity of the Marcan account reveals itself in the fact that the two acts are different in extent and viewpoints. The first is quite short; it is limited to the word of prayer, the breaking for distribution, and the figurative saying. The second contains the word of prayer, the distribution, the mention of the partaking, the figurative saying, the reference to the saving significance of his death, and the concluding eschatological saying. The comparison of the accounts shows that in the other accounts the two acts are increasingly harmonized with each other, both as to extent and in respect to the viewpoint which they contain. We obtain two parallel acts, in that the actions and words over the wine correspond exactly to those over the bread.

This harmonization takes place either by incorporating the component parts of the second act into the first (Matthew, Paul, Luke), or by abridging the second act on analogy with the first (Justin).

2. The Matthean Account (Matthew 26:26-29)

Matthew is on the way to harmonization. Through the φάγετε the explicit mention of the moment of partaking is incorporated into the first act. And since in the second act the invitation to partake also appears in place of the confirmation that they have partaken, the two acts correspond perfectly at this point. λάβετε, φάγετε· τοῦτό ἐστιν τὸ σῶμά μου. πίετε ἐξ αὐτοῦ πάντες· τοῦτο γάρ ἐστιν τὸ αἷμά μου. The harmonization is, however, not yet completely carried out. There is missing from the first act a reference corresponding to the saying about the significance of the shed blood (τὸ περὶ πολλῶν). Also the eschatological saying which concludes the figurative saying over the wine is not yet represented in connection with the bread.

Moreover, the πάντες which remains in the second act shows that here a confirmation has been transformed into an invitation. In connection with the confirmation it of course must be said that they all drank from it. In connection with the invitation, however, the πάντες is self-evident; or—if it is supposed to accentuate emphatically the solemnity of the invitation—how then can it be missing in connection with the bread? Here it would really be required, since Jesus cannot assume without further ado that all will actually eat the little piece of bread which he offers to them, whereas he follows with his eye the passing around of the cup. From Paul, Luke, and Justin, then, the πάντες is actually omitted as no longer of any consequence.

The connection of the concluding eschatological saying with the cup-saying, looking backward to it, and with the departure, looking forward to the way of passion, is still preserved by Matthew. Nevertheless the eschatological saying is no longer connected with the cup-saying by the forceful ἀμήν to accentuate the climax of the supper, so as to form the high point of the entire celebration, as in Mark, but it is only a closing remark, subordinated by means of δέ (Mark: ἀμὴν λέγω ὑμῖν; Matthew: λέγω δὲ ὑμῖν).

Thus for Matthew the process of harmonization is still in flux. For Paul it has already progressed much further.

3. The Pauline Account (1 Corinthians 11:23-26)

After each act is attached by way of conclusion: τοῦτο ποιεῖτε εἰς τὴν ἐμὴν ἀνάμνησιν. The first act is conformed to the second by the transferal of the phrase which refers to the meaning of the death, τὸ ὑπὲρ ὑμῶν. Only the ἔκλασεν has no parallel.

In Mark and Matthew the saying about the reunion at the meal in the future kingdom forms the conclusion to the saying over the cup. It only appears to have been omitted by Paul. Rather he presupposes it as the conclusion of both acts: ὁσάκις γὰρ ἐὰν ἐσθίητε τὸν ἄρτον τοῦτον καὶ τὸ ποτήριον πίνητε, τὸν θάνατον τοῦ κυρίου καταγγέλλετε, ἄχρι οὗ ἔλθῃ (verse 26).

"Till he come"—these words express the expectation of his coming and of the irruption of the kingdom. We must not disregard this expectation when we explain τοῦτο ποιεῖτε εἰς τὴν ἐμὴν ἀνάμνησιν. Accordingly the ἀνάμνησις has a double aspect: looking backward, it is a remembrance of Jesus' death; looking forward, it is a reminder of his parousia. The celebration is concerned with the crucified one, who will be revealed as Messiah at his coming, an office to which he is now already exalted by his resurrection to the right hand of God.

If we now consider the fact that the historical relation of the concluding eschatological saying has been lost so far as the second act is concerned, but that according to Paul's conception both acts are linked with the expectation of the parousia, then it is only natural to see in the τοῦτο ποιεῖτε—understood as a confirmation or as a command of repetition—the Pauline form of the concluding eschatological saying concealed in both acts.

For the first act, this is an artificial combination, since historically this reference to the parousia is connected only with the cup-saying, where the partaking is confirmed. The first act with its ἔκλασεν is not at all concerned about this expectation. Out of this situation there arises in Paul an intolerable grammatical confusion. The parallel to the ὁσάκις ἐὰν πίνητε, the expected ὁσάκις ἐὰν ἐσθίητε, is missing from the form of the τοῦτο ποιεῖτε in verse 24. Therefore the ποιεῖν in the first act can be understood as referring only to the breaking just referred to. But it follows from verses 25 and 26 that, corresponding to the ποιεῖν of the second act, the partaking, namely the eating, must be understood as meant by the ποιεῖν of the first act. Grammatically, only this would be justified: as often as you break this bread and drink this cup. In fact, however, it is supposed to mean: as often as you eat this bread. So too is the γάρ to be understood, which links verse 26 with verses 24 and 25 at the same time, so far as it presupposes the eating

52

and drinking as repetition of the action intended there by Jesus.

The harmonization is therefore achieved in spite of the latent opposition of the first act. The eschatological reference and the saying about the saving significance of the death are joined to both figurative sayings.

In this way Paul avoids a great difficulty through the form in which he presents this eschatological reference. In the original form this saying is a concluding saying. But if in this form it were attached to the first act, then the action would be split asunder in the middle, since then Jesus would conclude the celebration already with the bread. Luke felt this difficulty as he undertook to transfer the Pauline conception to the synoptic account.

4. The Lucan Account (Luke 22:14-20)

In the first place, Luke gives the concluding eschatological saying in direct discourse for both acts. For the cup saying, the form of the earlier Synoptics was available. He takes the Matthean form because Luke presupposes the invitation to partake, which Paul does not offer. By omitting the saying about the blood, Luke produces the following cup-saying (Luke 22:17-18): καὶ δεξάμενος ποτήριον εὐχαριστήσας εἶπεν· λάβετε τοῦτο καὶ διαμερίσατε εἰς ἑαυτούς· λέγω γὰρ ὑμῖν ὅτι οὐ μὴ πίω ἀπὸ τοῦ νῦν ἀπὸ τοῦ γενήματος τῆς ἀμπέλου ἕως ὅτου ἡ βασιλεία τοῦ θεοῦ ἔλθη.

Luke's attempt works out well. The διαμερίσατε had to be added so as not to anticipate the offering of the cup which follows later (verse 20). In this exigency the γάρ which has been inserted produces, in connection with the διαμερίσατε, a logical train of thought. The καινόν (cf. Matthew 26:29) was better omitted, because this adjective appears later as an explanatory addition to διαθήκη. The hue of the eschatological statement is somewhat faded (Matthew: ἕως τῆς ἡμέρας ἐκείνης ὅταν αὐτὸ πίνω μεθ' ὑμῶν καινὸν ἐν τῇ βασιλείᾳ τοῦ πατρός μου· Luke: ἕως ὅτου ἡ βασιλεία τοῦ θεοῦ ἔλθη).

It was more difficult for Luke to formulate the concluding eschatological saying for the first act, since here no material was available for him to shape, and the saying over the bread had already in Paul sufficiently demonstrated its resistance to being forcefully connected with any kind of eschatological reference. Only one way out was available: to refer the concluding eschatological saying to the entire meal, since this saying was required once for the action of eating. This

conception receives support from the thought that perhaps the historical celebration was a Passover meal. Therefore the newly constructed
concluding eschatological saying for the eating refers in Luke to the
Passover meal, which Jesus celebrates with his own. 15 καὶ εἶπεν πρὸς   54
αὐτούς· ἐπιθυμίᾳ ἐπεθύμησα τοῦτο τὸ πάσχα φαγεῖν μεθ᾽ ὑμῶν πρὸ
τοῦ με παθεῖν· 16 λέγω γὰρ ὑμῖν ὅτι οὐ μὴ φάγω αὐτὸ ἕως ὅτου
πληρωθῇ ἐν τῇ βασιλείᾳ τοῦ θεοῦ.

Luke's utilization of the Passover idea enables him to depict a meal
celebration at which the eating as well as the drinking receives an
eschatological reference. But by this procedure the historical celebration is torn asunder! First come the two eschatological sayings; they
are moved into the course of the Passover meal. The first saying forms
at the same time an impressive introduction, which does not at all
anticipate the saying over the bread: only with the saying over the cup
is there any difficulty. In order to contrast accurately the cup-saying,
which then appears with the actual historical celebration, with the
preceding cup-saying which was spoken during the course of the
Passover meal, it is reported in the Pauline form: τὸ ποτήριον μετὰ τὸ
δειπνῆσαι λέγων· τοῦτο τὸ ποτήριον ἡ καινὴ διαθήκη ἐν τῷ αἵματί
μου. The agreement continues this far. Now, however, the eschatological reference according to Paul (1 Corinthians 11:24-25: τοῦτο ποιεῖτε
etc.) has already been used with the Passover cup-saying, therefore
Luke here modulates back to Matthew and inserts τὸ ὑπὲρ ὑμῶν
ἐκχυννόμενον. For this reason the old Synoptic ἐν τῷ αἵματί μου
appeared already in place of the Pauline ἐν τῷ ἐμῷ αἵματί.

The first act is described according to Paul. From the Synoptics the
explicit mention of the offering (ἔδωκεν-διδόμενον) has forced its way
in. The τοῦτο ποιεῖτε has remained because the eschatological saying
in respect to the eating refers to the Passover meal in general.

Luke's account is explained literarily simply as an attempt to carry
back into the Synoptic historical narrative the harmonization of the
two acts attained by Paul, with the help obtained by connecting the
historical celebration with the Passover meal. This attempt, then,
results in the following course of the celebration: at the beginning of
the Passover meal Jesus indicates that he will celebrate it again with
the disciples only in the kingdom of God. He repeats such a statement
when the cup is passed around the first time. With the offering of the
bread in the course of the celebration he speaks the figurative saying
about his body, and likewise over the cup the figurative saying about

55 his blood. Both acts are absolutely the same through their stress upon the saving value of the sacrifice (verse 19: τὸ ὑπὲρ ὑμῶν διδόμενον; verse 20: τὸ ὑπὲρ ὑμῶν ἐκχυννόμενον). Even this harmonization is not accomplished without stylistic roughness, for in the second act a poured-out cup is spoken of, whereas the blood is meant.

As with Paul, both acts are concluded by the τοῦτο ποιεῖτε. We have, therefore, a harmonization which extends even to the measured rhythm of the language. To be sure, in the process the conclusion of the celebration has disappeared. The stately saying about drinking again in the Father's kingdom was already used at the beginning of the Passover celebration, instead of, as in Mark and Matthew, forming the transition to the departure. In its place Luke has the episodes about the designation of the betrayer, the dispute about greatness, and the prophecy of Peter's denial (Luke 22:21-38). As a result, Luke omits the portrayal of the solemn departure after the singing of a hymn (Mark 14:26 = Matthew 26:30). "He went, as his custom was, to the Mount of Olives" (Luke 22:39: καὶ ἐξελθὼν ἐπορεύθη κατὰ τὸ ἔθος εἰς τὸ ὄρος τῶν ἐλαιῶν).

An original conception of the essence of the historical celebration does not lie at the basis of this representation. In no case does it result from the attempt to give a historical basis to the separation of the "Lord's Supper" from the common religious meal, for which Paul is supposed to have prepared the way! This formless account is to be explained only on the basis of the principle παρηκολουθηκότι ἄνωθεν πᾶσιν ἀκριβῶς καθεξῆς γράψαι (Luke 1:3).

It is, therefore, not to be expected that, by deletion or by transposition of verses, an account can be obtained from the Lucan representation which goes back to an original, earlier conception of the historical celebration. More than through such attempts, we do justice to the value of the Lucan representation if we appreciate the literary skill, the aesthetic sensitivity, and the liturgical warmth to which this portrayal bears witness.

5. The Justinian Account *(1 Apologia 66)*

Here the harmonization is accomplished by abridging the second act on analogy with the first. The celebration reported is limited to two puzzling sayings of Jesus. After a prayer of thanksgiving over the bread, he says: "this is my body"; in like manner over the cup: "this is my blood" (τὸν Ἰησοῦν λαβόντα ἄρτον εὐχαριστήσαντα εἰπεῖν·

τοῦτο ποιεῖτε εἰς τὴν ἀνάμνησίν μου, τοῦτό ἐστι τὸ σῶμά μου. καὶ τὸ   56
ποτήριον ὁμοίως λαβόντα καὶ εὐχαριστήσαντα εἰπεῖν· τοῦτό ἐστι τὸ
αἷμά μου).

There are missing the breaking of the bread, the reference to the value of the sacrifice, and the accentuation of the expected or ensuing partaking in the second act. The concluding eschatological saying is also omitted. Only in the first act is the τοῦτο ποιεῖτε found in the Pauline form, but Paul's τὴν ἐμὴν ἀνάμνησίν (1 Corinthians 11:24) has become τὴν ἀνάμνησίν μου.

Here, however, the opposition of the first act to an interpolation of this kind is intensified to the point of intolerability. To what is the ποιεῖν supposed to refer? To the preceding word of prayer? The breaking is not mentioned. The partaking is presupposed, but not accentuated. So far as the grammatical exposition is concerned, the τοῦτο ποιεῖτε here is thus meaningless, and the fact that it is mentioned only in the first act is unintelligible.

This abbreviated representation has lost interest in the entire historical situation. To be sure, Justin, *Dialogue* 41, 70, and 117 mentions that, in the congregational celebration, remembrance of Jesus' death also plays a role. In Justin's account, however, there is no indication that this meal took place the night before Jesus' death.

From "the Justinian account" alone we would, therefore, know only that Jesus at a meal, after he had offered a prayer of thanksgiving over the bread, had commanded his disciples to observe this custom in memory of him. Continuing after that, he designated the bread which he had blessed as his body and the cup which he had blessed as his blood.

Chapter XIII

The Authenticity of the Marcan Account

1. The Proof

An account is authentic which in no way is influenced by the conception of the congregational celebration. The Marcan account is authentic because it meets this test.

What is the basis of the harmonization of the two acts, which all other accounts, in contrast to Mark, exhibit, even though they vary from one another in manner and degree? In the influence which the early Christian celebration exercises on the conception of the histori- cal celebration. The congregational celebration was a meal in which the same significance was attributed to the eating as to the drinking. Quite naturally this understanding was transferred to the historical celebration. Nothing else was known than that Jesus must have acted and spoken in perfectly corresponding ways over the bread and wine, inasmuch as in the derived celebration the same value was attributed to the eating as to the drinking. In this way the primitive Christian celebration required that the two acts of the historical celebration be harmonized with each other.

If we did not now possess the Marcan account, we would not find anything unusual about the similarity of the two acts, since this similarity also appears to our perception as the most natural. All modern attempts to reconstruct the "original words of institution" likewise advocate harmonization. We therefore are also inclined to regard the similarity of the two acts as self-evident, without further ado.

Now, however, the Marcan account shows that the similarity of the two acts is not self-evident. It is, therefore, necessary to seek an explanation either for the dissimilarity of the two acts in Mark or for the similarity in the other accounts. In doing so it happens that we can indeed derive the others from the Marcan account, but not vice versa. Matthew and Paul—the Lucan account is a pure literary product— represent the celebration according to the second act of Mark, Justin according to the first. If we make appropriate allowance for the harmonization of both acts in each account—a harmonization which is indicated by grammatical roughnesses and impossibilities—then each time we obtain the Marcan account.

At the same time a certain development is shown in the harmonization of the two acts. That Matthew has not completely carried out this harmonization allows us to recognize that the similarity of the acts is not original. Therefore this similarity must be based on the historical perspective of the early period which formulated these accounts. Since this basis can be given only in the meal-character of the congregational celebration which harmonized the eating and the drinking, it is quite certain that these accounts have gone through the medium of the early Christian interpretation of the congregational celebration. Mark stands outside of this process, because he does not exhibit the harmonization. Therefore Mark is authentic.

58   That the conception of the historical celebration in Paul and Justin is affected to a very high degree by the conception of the congregational celebration is obvious. For them the historical account is only a means to an end. The historical account is supposed to advocate a definite view of the congregational celebration. The manner in which they relate the two accounts far surpasses our comprehension. We always understand the congregational celebration only as a corre-

sponding repetition of the historical celebration, insofar as the former is based on the latter. Paul and Justin identify the two, in that they let the congregational celebration be given with the historical celebration. As a result, trains of thought arise which are quite surprising to us.

First Corinthians 11:26 raises the question. In verses 24 and 25 Jesus carries out the institution. Who is speaking in verse 26? The γάρ, insofar as it is causally related to the preceding, excludes a change of subject. The expression τὸν θάνατον τοῦ κυρίου shows, however, that the historical situation is left behind and Paul is speaking of the congregational celebration. But for this purpose the γάρ is not suitable, for that which concerns the congregational celebration is not a foundation on the words of Jesus, but an inference from the historical saying. In this sentence Paul, therefore, so carries out the transition from the historical celebration to the congregational celebration that for a moment he, as it were, pushes the two together.

For that reason he fuses together two sentences, of which the first pertains to the historical situation, the second to the explanation of the congregational celebration.

1. Jesus to the disciples at the close of the figurative sayings: "for (γάρ) as often as you eat this bread and drink this wine, you proclaim my death, until I come."

2. Paul explaining to the church the essence of its celebration on the basis of the historical celebration: "Therefore (ὥστε), as often as you eat this bread and drink this wine, you proclaim the Lord's death, until he come."

Justin offers a companion-piece to this striking transition. In the famous exposition of *1 Apologia* 65 and 66 he summarizes the historical celebration and the congregational celebration in a common expression, in that he designates them as: ἡ δι'εὐχῆς λόγου τοῦ παρ' αὐτοῦ (sc. Jesus) εὐχαριστηθεῖσα τροφή. This expression gives evidence of an identification of the two celebrations, which goes far beyond our concept of the appropriate repetition. The food at the congregational celebration is, as at the historical celebration, consecrated by a word of prayer from Jesus. There is, therefore, no difference.

What the harmonization of the two acts indicates is confirmed by the argumentation with which Paul and Justin connect the congregational celebration with the historical celebration: they see the historical celebration only in light of the congregational celebration.

So long as the comparison of texts aimed exclusively at discovering the most probable and most appropriate form of the words of institution, the conception of the possibility of a Pauline or a Justinian special tradition was legitimate, since both offered the "words of institution" in forms which are both independent of each other and which are basically different from the two earlier Synoptics. If, however, we examine the accounts as accounts, and if we ask them, without listening to alluring praises of their "words of institution," what they know about the course and the essence of the entire historical procedure at which these figurative sayings were spoken, then that is the end of the apparent originality. We see that they conceive of the historical celebration according to the congregational celebration which was familiar to them, except that Jesus at it distributes food and drink and speaks the well-known figurative sayings. Therefore their conception of "the words of institution" does not go back to a Pauline or a Justinian special tradition, but it is to be explained historically on the basis of the presupposed congregational celebration. Paul and Justin differ in their "words of institution," because and insofar as the Justinian congregational celebration differs from the Pauline congregational celebration. Between the two a change in the interpretation of the celebration must have taken place.

Thus the new formulation of the problem brings with it a new interpretation of authenticity, which is no longer founded on opinions but on laws. What we now regard as authentic is not the shortest or apparently clearest report of "the words of institution" but the representation of the total historical procedure, for which an influence by the congregational celebration cannot be proved, whether or not the "formula of institution" in question suits our taste.

Previously it was regarded as interesting to set forth, with a certain skeptical nonchalance, the proposition that we can never know anything concerning the authenticity of the accounts. Even if there was a more authentic account among our accounts, still we did not have any means of discovering it among the others. Through the new conception of authenticity this skepticism is eliminated. We do possess one authentic account. Anyone who will dispute this claim must prove that the Markan account is a fantasy-product disavowed by the other representations. Authentic or meaningless: that is the only available alternative.

60

2. The Consequences of the Authenticity of the Marcan Account

The new interpretation of authenticity marks the first success of the new formulation of the problem. It opens the way for the new attempt at a solution. Jesus invited the disciples to eat his body and to drink his blood: this supposed common state of affairs of all accounts seemed to block the way. Through the authenticity of the Marcan account, however, this apparent state of affairs is invalidated. That which was decided on the basis of the criticism of modern interpretations is historically confirmed: Jesus did not invite the disciples to partake of his body and his blood, but he spoke the figurative sayings during the course of the partaking, not before. The saying over the cup comes only after all have drunk.

Therefore we have one account in which the essence of the celebration is based, not on the figurative sayings, but on the solemn proceedings. This discovery required that the problem be formulated anew. Now it has become a fact. Therefore the problem of the Lord's Supper is solvable for historical criticism.

3. The Secrets of the Messiahship and of the Passion in the Lord's Supper

The significance of the offering of the elements to be partaken of remains puzzling for the time being. Only the negative is clear, namely, that the figurative sayings must not be explained on the basis of the symbolical action of the breaking and of the presupposed pouring out of the wine. The moment of presentation plays no role in the accounts and finally disappears completely, as the Justinian text shows, where the breaking is not mentioned at all.

If we want to explain the figurative sayings according to the authentic Marcan text, then we must explain the first on the basis of the breaking, the second on the basis of the fact that all disciples have drunk. We would, therefore, obtain two figurative sayings which are constituted entirely differently.

The figurative sayings about the body and blood must, however, somehow contain the concept of the passion. That Jesus by means of these figurative sayings expressed for the final time the secret of his passion is given in the circumstances of this last meeting. Therefore if we are not able to understand the figurative sayings correctly, it is because we erroneously conceive the secret of the passion.

Now it is the peculiarity of all modern historical interpretations of the Lord's Supper that they do not stress the eschatological thought in the celebration. They do not utilize the saying about drinking the new wine in the Father's kingdom as a statement which constitutes the essence of the final meal, but at the most they make out of it a supplementary saying.

In the Marcan text, however, this eschatological saying assumes a principal position. It is the concluding saying of the celebration, spoken solemnly and impressively. At the same time it is closely and inseparably connected with the saying about the shed blood, so that it seems to form with it one single thought. This close connection between the ideas of death and return is characteristic of the second act in Mark.

But we also meet the same connection in Paul, and to be sure in both acts. According to him—and in the process he expressly appeals to the historical occurrence—the significance of the eating and drinking consists somehow in the proclamation of the death of the Lord together with the expectation of his parousia. "As often as you eat this bread and drink this wine, you do proclaim the Lord's death until he come."

In both the authentic account of the historical celebration and in the oldest account of the congregational celebration we have, therefore, an organic connection between the concept of the passion and the eschatological expectation. It is thus incorrect to find the essence of the celebration only in the last utterance of the concept of death. Jesus did not speak to his own of his death but of his death and of his speedy reunion with them at the meal in the new kingdom. The secret of his death, which at this celebration was expressed by Jesus for the final time in the most moving and impressive manner, contains the concept of the passion in the closest connection with the eschatological expectation.

62

The modern historical interpretations of the Lord's Supper are, therefore, unhistorical, because the concept of the passion with which they operate exhibits no connection with eschatology. Therefore they cannot express the essential feature of the historical celebration and of the earliest congregational celebration. In order to grasp the essence of the final meal, a glance is therefore necessary into the eschatological character of Jesus' secret of the passion. This secret cannot be extracted from the celebration itself, since Jesus there expresses the secret in a figurative saying. We are not, however, able to explain the figurative saying.

At the final meal Jesus acts as Messiah, and to be sure as suffering Messiah. If we do not understand his action, it is because we wrongly understand the secrets of his messiahship and passion. The Lord's Supper can be understood only on the basis of the general pattern of the life of Jesus. Our interpretations of the Lord's Supper are erroneous; therefore the interpretation of the life of Jesus which has led us to these interpretations of the Supper are also erroneous.

The problem of the Lord's Supper is the problem of the life of Jesus! A new interpretation of the Lord's Supper can be built only upon a new interpretation of the life of Jesus, an interpretation which so contains the secrets of the messiahship and of the passion that his solemn action at the final meal becomes comprehensible and understandable. A new life of Jesus: that is the only way to the solution of the problem of the Lord's Supper.

Indexes

(For reference to particular subjects, see the extensive table of contents, pages v-viii.)

Index of Persons

(Page numbers in italics indicate brief biographical references—by Schweitzer himself or by the editor—or references to a specific influence upon Schweitzer's study of the problem of the Lord's Supper.)

Index of Texts

(Page numbers in italics indicate substantive treatments of the major texts.)